GUIDED

GUIDED

JOURNEY INTO THE UNKNOWN
TO AWAKEN THE SOUL
AND LIVE IN TRUTH

SIRI K. ZEMEL, PHD

JACOBS HOUSE PUBLISHING

COPYRIGHT © 2021 SIRI K. ZEMEL
All rights reserved.

GUIDED
Journey into the Unknown to Awaken the Soul and Live in Truth

ISBN	978-1-5445-2064-3	*Hardcover*
	978-1-5445-2063-6	*Paperback*
	978-1-5445-2062-9	*Ebook*
	978-1-5445-2065-0	*Audiobook*

Cover designer: Liz Driesbach

Dedicated to those in hiding.
You are not alone.

CONTENTS

PART 1

Note to Reader: Background and Semantics   XIII
Introduction: Shaking Loose   XIX

PART 2

1. Bridging Across Dimensions   3
   Receiving Support   *3*
   Lifting the Veil   *7*
   Communicating with the Soul   *10*
   Practicing Meditation   *14*

2. Healing the Protective Layers of the Heart   17
Tuning In   17
Softening a Wounded Heart   22
Finding Security in the Non-Self   30
Slowing Down to Feel   34

3. Opening to Consciousness   39
Allowing the Flow   39
Having Fun Along the Way   45
Listening to the Body   48
Engaging the Intellect   50

4. Shifting Disconnection to Interconnection   53
Surrendering to the Great Partnership   53
Getting Out of the Way   58
Unlocking the Psyche   60
Connecting with Truth   63

5. Awakening the Indestructible Soul   71
Coming Out of Hiding   71
Choosing Joy and Love   77
Remaining Humble   91
Bathing in the Light   97

PART 3

Stories and Perspectives 107

Annie: Connecting with My Parents *108*

Michael: Perspectives as a Scientist, Jew and Witness *114*

Paula: Through the Eyes of a Christian Mother *118*

Kerry: Telling My Secret to Our Grandmother *124*

Social Responsibilities 145

Rational Questioning *145*

A Nascent Field *148*

Conclusion: One Beautiful and Awkward Day at a Time 151

Acknowledgements 159

Recommended Readings 163

About the Author 169

NOTE TO READER

BACKGROUND AND SEMANTICS

This book invites the reader to journey into the unknown, which may require surrender and psychological flexibility. The mystical-psychic phenomena presented herein are curiously pluralistic and paradoxical. This is not a scientific text. Instead, it is a chronicle of spiritual and/or psychic awakening, full of debate and struggle. The details of this story may be unique, though fighting the inner battle of self-acceptance and individuation is a human right of passage. Similarly, the decision to uncover and ultimately unleash hidden parts of the self is something that many, if not all of us, are faced with at some point in life. This is an adventure that demands wholehearted courage. If such a surrender proves difficult, you are in good company. It took me decades, despite a progressive education, an eclectic worldview, and a dedication to personal development.

Following undergraduate and graduate degrees in nutrition science, my doctorate work in mind-body medicine expanded my conviction in the power of meditation, the value of the placebo effect and imagery in healing, the plasticity of the brain, the inherent intelligence of the nervous system, and the need for human connection in emotional restoration and healing. Using the lens of classic grounded theory for my dissertation taught me the richest answers often lie beyond the questions we know to ask. My last eighteen years of professional experience in nutrition, eating disorders, addiction, mental health, and behavioral medicine have shown me that the mind and body (each separately and together) hold an innate, intricate, and astonishing ability to move towards healing and wholeness.

The mystical concepts shared in this book have existed for many thousands of years across many world cultures and religions, though this book does not aim to defend these phenomena. While these experiences felt absolutely real to me, I have included a brief section towards the end of this book on rational questioning, social responsibilities, and

— NOTE TO READER —

recommended readings for further exploration. Otherwise, the following chapters move through my own guided journey, toggling between trance-induced channeled messages and ordinary states of consciousness. Throughout the book, I use italics to delineate mediated accounts and experiences.

The channeled and interpreted messages herein did not originate from my conscious mind but from prayerful altered states of consciousness accessed through just a few deep breaths and nothing more. Some may believe that each of us holds the ability to receive guidance from a nonphysical, spiritual dimension. Others may believe these paranormal experiences can be explained as a resourceful psyche (either through an adaptive creative imagination or a maladaptive dissociative identity). I have suspended full cognitive understanding to receive the extraordinary benefits of these passages into the unknown.

Regarding the communications themselves, the following chapters present actual transcriptions from interpreted tongue-speak over a ten-year period. I have only edited the transcriptions to be grammatically cohesive—I have distilled broken, English-tongue-speak sputtering to only the English, correcting the sentence fragments and duplicate wording. Overall, I consider myself to be the organizer of this work, but not its original source. A few people who have shared and witnessed this expedition with me each offer their own views towards the end of this book: my best friend, Dr. Annie Wills; my husband, Dr. Michael Zemel; my mother, Paula Jacobs; and my sister, Kerry Page.

Regarding semantics, I am sensitive to the perspectives of various faiths and belief systems (including agnostics, atheists, Christians, Jews, Sikhs, and others), so I invite the exchange of any offensive words presented to others that would be most comfortable and accessible in the reader's mind. Terms used throughout the text include *Source*, *God*, *Creator*, the *All That Is*, *the flow*, and *the universe*, just as these words channeled through me.

The concept of tongue-speak is referenced throughout this book, although my encounters with an enigmatic dialect do not fit into the most commonly understood description of this phenomenon. Speaking in tongues is a commonly accepted expression of faith in the charismatic Christian and Pentecostal religions. Though raised Catholic as a child, I have not practiced any form of Christianity for the last twenty-five years. I have never attended a church where tongue-speaking occurred, nor have I ever been in the presence of another person possessing this gift. Tongue-speak emerged as inherent from within, rather than learned or modeled.

— NOTE TO READER —

Finally, the word shamanism is used throughout this book to describe traversing in and out of otherworldly trance states. I do not claim to be a shaman in the way it is most commonly understood—as an ancient and indigenous honor bestowed upon a designated spiritual leader. I have never met or worked with a shaman, and I have never visited a shamanic community. This ability to access both the spiritual and physical worlds emerged as inherent from within, rather than learned or modeled.

With these perspectives in mind and with an adventurous spirit, let us cross over the threshold and journey into the unknown.

INTRODUCTION

SHAKING LOOSE

We often played together on the old wooden floors of my tiny childhood bedroom, overseen by Irish-Catholic blessings on the walls. My imaginary friends and I communicated through an encrypted language that was all our own. While growing up, this dialect automatically poured out of me if I became startled or awakened in the middle of the night (much to my embarrassment and to the laughter of my siblings). One grade school slumber party haunted me for years after I sat up in my sleep and spoke "my language" out loud, which was gibberish to anyone listening.

I was the one odd sister (out of four) who loved our Catholic school education. I felt connected to angels, saints, and the ideas of goodness and heaven. My teenage years brought curiosity and expansion. I fell in love with all things mind-expanding: poetry, marijuana, LSD, yoga, meditation, and the search for truth. In my twenties, I converted to Sikhism (a monotheistic religion from India) and spent many hours controlling my breath, chanting ancient languages, and holding yogic postures to attain spiritual union. In my undergrad and graduate years at the University of Tennessee, I was deeply immersed in nutrition, dance, physiology, and psychology, yet the enigmatic flow of sounds continued through me when I was alone and relaxed. I loved to sing my strange heart song. I felt a sense of peace when I allowed the harmonious melody to flow through me, though I never dared to share it with others.

After a graduate degree, a second marriage, and two adorable children, the language intensified. I was in a non-traditional marriage with a deeply devout Jew named Michael, and I enjoyed going to synagogue with him on occasion. I always believed God to be bigger than religion, and any house of worship offered the same opportunity for divine connection. Sometimes, when my soul's voice longed to be expressed, and while the congregation prayed in Hebrew, I wandered down the hall into the small empty sanctuary that was lit by a single stained-glass window on one side. Here, in the quiet darkness, the words sang through me, filling me with peace.

I was young in my career as a nutritionist, and one afternoon as I was preparing to teach a weight management class, I sensed an ethereal presence around me. This feeling stayed with me for several weeks. It was with me when I walked in the neighborhood, picked the kids up from school, and folded laundry at home. I finally asked out loud, "Who are you?" The response felt like glitter and delight as I heard the reply. A voice within me, but not from me, responded, "Gabriel." Was this "the" Gabriel? The angel? Surely not. Not knowing what to think about this visitation, I tucked it away and said nothing.

A few years later, I was directing eating disorder treatment centers hundreds of miles apart. Frequent travel, work responsibilities, and mothering my young children led me to seek regular massages to rebalance. I remember lying on a heated table, slipping into tranquility. The peaceful pale blue walls and the smell of lavender on the sheets guided me into full relaxation. As soon as my body let go and melted into the massage table, an uncontrollable shaking emanated from my core, and that old familiar language bubbled to the surface. After a brief, embarrassing conversation with the massage therapist, I willed myself to push whatever it was deep inside.

Truthfully, this was happening a lot more lately, each time I quieted my buzzing and frenetic state. My body quivered during moments of deeply relaxed meditation and as I'd lie down to fall asleep most nights. This uninvited trembling was accompanied by the urge to spout the flow of unknown words that surfaced repeatedly. It felt like something was trying to get my attention, but I had no idea what it was or what to do about it.

One late summer night, after a sensual connection with my husband, the utterings poured across my lips for nearly an hour with a fierce passion and sense of importance. It was like the sex had jostled something loose—a buried force, refusing constraint any longer. Sitting upright in my bed, naked and keenly aware, I suddenly felt a nonphysical presence enter the room. What felt like an old and loving spirit approached as a whitish-translucent orb. To my surprise, she came close, reached in, and stretched out my third eye to the size of a bowling ball, creating a huge opening in the center of my forehead. A larger-than-life stream of energy descended into me, which I can only describe as the midnight starry-blue substance I had seen in my deepest meditations. The strange dialect harmoniously sang through me, enveloping me with absolute tranquility and bliss. "Who are you?" I asked. "I am you," she replied. Tears of overwhelming awe rolled down my cheeks. Michael slept soundly next to me, unaware that anything had occurred.

I had never received a mental health diagnosis other than mild postpartum depression, and I had stopped using mind-altering substances over a decade prior. But just to cover all bases, I reached out to a licensed mental health professional for a consult. We both agreed this was a sacred and benevolent experience worth exploring.

Curious and open, I studied with Dr. Brian Weiss, an internationally recognized psychiatrist who teaches past life regression therapy to professionals and has published numerous books on the topic. His writings roused my soul. The stories about the soul's journey across lifetimes pulled me into a kind of remembering—the kind of remembering when something is calling you, but you can't quite put your finger on it.

At my second professional training with Brian Weiss at the Omega Institute in Rhinebeck, New York, I found myself in a small group with therapists, doctors, and other professionals. It was my turn to enter the relaxed, hypnotic trance state. Instead of recalling a past life memory like my colleagues in the group, my weird, distinctive language spilled out. Dr. Weiss analyzed the dialect, and it was not any language he had come across in his work or travels. He did not believe this to be *xenoglossy*, a paranormal phenomenon in which a person spontaneously speaks a foreign language without having known that language in the current lifetime. Dr. Weiss spoke of near-death experiences and deep meditative states—of connections with loving entities, such as spiritual guides and ascended masters. He spoke of mystics who could communicate with the other side. "Continue to explore it," he instructed.

Something definitely awakened within me, but I couldn't pinpoint it exactly. It was awkward, and I wanted to understand precisely what was happening. Seeking answers, I enrolled in a Mind-Body Medicine doctoral program at Saybrook University with Dr. James Gordon, an internationally recognized, Harvard-educated psychiatrist who teaches self-awareness and other mind-body practices all over the globe. This hybrid online-onsite program allowed me to continue working my full-time job while traveling to California once every semester to complete the course work.

In some of our earliest work together, Dr. Gordon introduced the healing power of experiential practices within small groups, including meditation, breathwork, dancing, and more. During one of the lively breathwork and dancing sessions, the physical trembling and passionate words again arose and poured out of me. Sensing my embarrassment, Dr. Gordon confidently created a safe space big enough to hold the formidable energy, and in so doing, he gave me a precious gift that day. He normalized the experience, which gave me the permission I needed to continue probing the mystery.

I wanted to decipher the indiscernible sounds that were moving across my lips. It took many months of practicing meditative trance before I could control the flow of the energy and the spouting of words. I ultimately learned to regulate my entrance into—and exit out of—this peaceful yet otherworldly state. Ultimately, I became able to process small bits of the cryptic content. This progression was slow, difficult, and felt as though my mind was condensing something beyond limit or comprehension down into the narrow neuronal pathways of cognition.

After several months of practice within a safely contained psychotherapeutic environment, I built and strengthened my resiliency to remain connected long enough to both receive and interpret full streams of communications. In this time, the entities dialoguing with me referred to themselves as "spiritual guides" and to these conversations as "my classroom." Full of doubt and trained in logical thinking, I challenged that assertion for many years, seeking other explanations.

The lessons taught were deeply compassionate, kind, and supportive, including clear guidance and instructions on how to live with greater happiness, love, and joy. Entering the mystical classroom filled me with a blissful ecstasy unlike any drug or physiological state imaginable. It was supreme. However, opening myself up to channel this intense energy also took a toll on my physical body. Coming back into my body after each session left me with a headache, nausea, and sheer exhaustion for the rest of the day.

Sometimes I stayed away from this work for many months, but whenever I did, the body shakes and pent-up tongue-speak still bubbled to the surface. This energetic force from within seemed to have a will of its own. I ultimately found that allowing whatever this was to move through me in a controlled way saved it from coming out on its own when I least expected it. So, I obediently carved out time to return to the numinous sanctuary as often as my academic, professional, and family responsibilities would allow.

This unusual education went on for several years in hiding, about once per week to once per month. Very few people knew my secret. During this time, I continued to raise my children, complete my doctorate, and advance my professional career. Over time, the physical convulsions and uncontrolled linguistic outbursts subsided completely. I published my dissertation on hungering rather than tongue-speaking because these celestial communications had become too sacred (and my belief still too fragile) for the brutal, unyielding analysis of academia. Deeply committed to my career as a behavioral healthcare executive, these ethereal experiences were like visitations to another world that just happened on weekends, after which I tightly buttoned up and returned to the hustle and bustle of my busy life.

A few of my closest friends sometimes asked me to communicate with the other side and even channel loved ones who had passed away. I enjoyed these practices and was happy to serve as a conduit of connection. However, I wasn't prepared to label myself as a spiritual medium. Publicly coming out with this part of myself threatened my professional credibility and the socially-accepted identity I had built as a driven, level-headed, data-based leader. Filled with self-criticism and doubt about this peculiar part of myself, I kept the phenomenon hidden.

I lived in two very different worlds for many years. An outer mask of normalcy covered up the secret I wasn't ready to let out. My marriage was strained. High doses of caffeine kept me racing through my days, and lidocaine patches kept back pain manageable. Sweet tasting, little reddish-brown pills erased tension headaches. The giant Advil bottle kept residence in my dim and messy bathroom closet, always standing ready to refill the purse-size bottle. It was so overused that it was devoid of any remaining color on the label. I ended most days with a glass of red wine (or often something stronger), binged Netflix, and munched on chocolate—all in an effort to numb out instead of facing my truth.

The shame of my cowardice and hypocrisy worsened the dynamic. For the last decade, I had taught meditation, nutrition, and self-awareness. I led teams of mental health professionals. I had a direct line to divine communications and a pretty decent tool kit of healthy coping skills. I knew what I needed to do, but it felt too hard to take that next step—to own and express all parts of myself, especially the hidden occult part.

The following chapters share this personal struggle, interwoven with transcriptions of channeled communications along the way. The messages over these years were clear and gentle. From a great unknown source, this book offers curious views on matters of the heart and psyche. It's

— SHAKING LOOSE —

a course towards surrender, self-acceptance, perception of the invisible, and a return to wholeness. I pray this story offers hope to other misfits like myself. From my weird heart to yours, enjoy the journey.

CHAPTER 1

BRIDGING ACROSS DIMENSIONS

RECEIVING SUPPORT

Each time I allowed the unknown words to express themselves, a sense of warmth filled me. A soft glowing light both surrounded me and emanated from within me all at once. A soothing, peaceful, and all-consuming wholeness signaled the connection was genuine. Time stood still, and I wanted to stay in this bubble for all of eternity. Unfortunately, the sensations didn't last forever. As soon as the tongue-speak subsided and I opened my eyes, awareness of my body and mind returned me to an ordinary state of consciousness. Though I didn't understand the meaning of the utterances, there was something unquestionably profound about connecting to this invisible realm.

I was early in my career while mothering my two beautiful, blonde-headed little girls—my biggest joys in life. My days were busy working with patients, facilitating nutrition and mindfulness groups, leading a small staff of healing professionals, and cooking wholesome meals for my young family. Despite a full and rich life, it felt like something was missing. A nagging in my soul and a literal shaking in my body continued to pull me towards the inexplicable dimension I recently learned to tap into. The blissful euphoria of being in that realm was unmatched, so of course, I wanted to keep going back to it.

I wanted validation that I was indeed not psychotic but mostly needed a method for decoding the messages, so I reached out to a therapist friend—we will call her Dianne. I asked if she would hold space for me to work with the language encounters. It was a bit of an unconventional request, but she agreed. I popped into her cozy office located just on the edge of downtown every couple of weeks. Once settled into her tan leather couch, I would close my eyes, exhale, and relax into the calm, peaceful state. After a few moments of quiet deep breathing, I would open my mouth and let the dialect flow out. The more I allowed the tongue-speak to express itself, the easier it became to control the flow of energy and information—the receiving and interpreting of the messages. Through this process, Dianne and I set the stage for each session to have a definitive beginning and end. This allowed me to enter and exit the all-consuming, out-of-body trance state in a safe and grounded way within a protected psychotherapeutic environment.

There is a great deal of spirit, of life force, that travels with you and within all of creation. You forget there are so many resources available to you. You do not have to understand or analyze it for it to affect you. The world will continue to unfold, even without your false sense of control. The burden you carry and the need to feel you are in control produces tension and worry that blocks the flow of God-consciousness, the universal vibration of the cosmos. Surrender. Your world is an illusion of separateness.

The more you allow yourself to open, the more soothing it will become for you, the more peace you will feel, and you will develop more trust that you are held. That begins at this moment by surrendering and receiving support and guidance—building that trust so we can dance in creation each moment, each day, together.

It is important for you to understand that we are your support, your entourage, your counsel, your spiritual guides, your guardian angels. No matter what you call us, we are still the same. We are the souls that move through this existence with you. Every person has support in this way. Some people mention lifting the veil. Some people use prayer or ritual to call upon spirits. It is all the same, and we are always here, whether you realize it or not, whether you lift the veil or not. It doesn't change the fact that we are here all the time.

Sometimes we influence your thoughts, ideas, insights, and intuitions. The more you call on us, the easier it is for you to receive guidance and direction from us. Please recognize that when you do not call on us, we stay out of the way. We watch out to offer safety and protection, but we do not operate outside of your will. A person must choose to ask for help. We are here, but if you do not want to activate us, then we stay in the background.

These were some of the early messages that came through mediated communications with the other side. Or maybe it wasn't the other side at all? Maybe it was just an illusion of separation. Either way, I definitely had more questions than answers. How was this working? Was I really interacting with angelic guides? Or was my mind more imaginative than I realized?

LIFTING THE VEIL

Professionally, I was directing eating disorder clinics located several hundred miles apart. My evening and weekend doctorate studies in integrative medicine included guided imagery, hypnosis, trance work, and other related areas to deepen my understanding of the mind in healing. Deeply steeped in the intellectual side of academia, carving out time to practice these techniques amidst child-raising, full-time work, and travel was limited. Likewise, my unexplained mystical explorations fell far down the priority list at this point. I would go several months without "coming to class." In these periods of time, my body's shaking would resurface, and the pent-up tongue-speak bubbled to the surface. It was as if this force had a will of its own, expressing itself however it could. But I was far too busy to bother with that now. Spiritually, I remained blind.

What do you think it means to lift the veil? It means you have a cover over your eyes. Not the eyes that allow you to physically see the world, but your soul and your connection with us. Oh, how difficult it is to be human and experience a blinded reality. Your perception is so limited. The veil is part of the earthly design—the blind environment is part of your learning. Even though you do not see, part of you knows, feels, receives, and is connected to everything that is happening. There is a vast transfer of energy and consciousness happening in every moment. When you close your eyes, and when you consciously connect with the energy that moves through your body, you can heighten your attunement. Your job now is to slow down and remember that you can connect to see the unseen, to hear the unheard, and perceive how energy is moving beyond the physical level. You must remember you are not totally blind—you have access to knowledge, answers, and guidance. Feeling stuck and without information is an illusion. Move out of your head. Move out of trying to control things. Let go.

Calling on the relationship with us and allowing healing energy to move through you is not supernatural or extraordinary. It is a natural part of human existence. When you live in harmony with the physical and spiritual, you see a fuller picture of yourself, of life, and of creation. You can receive a knowing, feeling, or a subtle shift in energy, in which you can perceive and experience the physical world slightly differently. This gives you a fuller picture and a deeper understanding of this world as your classroom. There is no separation. You see from the perspective of your personality, experiences, thoughts, fears, and feelings. Yet when you perceive a separation or duality, that is a glimpse into the layers of the ego's protection. The oneness of spiritual and physical integration can happen when the barriers of the ego dissolve. In this state, it is easier to see beauty, to feel love, experience joy, and remember the lightness of the soul.

One day, Dianne asked if I could connect with her mentor, who had just passed away that week. His name was Bobby Drinnon, and he had been a local psychic intuitive. I had never met him, and I had no idea if I could communicate with a departed soul. After praying for guidance and protection, I allowed the linguistic flow to transport me. Bobby appeared right away, and I perceived him through closed eyes. He was brilliantly lit and accompanied by an equally luminescent angelic companion. Bobby was absolutely glowing, buoyant, and filled with joy. He had the excitement of a little kid. My friend asked him questions (through me), and Bobby answered (through me) as if the three of us were actually together in the same room.

I had connected with a force, an energy, and a beautiful spirit-filled world, but I wasn't sure how to frame this experience in my mind. Was this heavenly dimension legitimate, or was it a fantasy of my imagination? This was a lot to grapple with, and I still needed answers.

COMMUNICATING WITH THE SOUL

One of my closest friends, Annie, also loved sharing these transcendent explorations with me. Annie had flowing silver hair and a smile that could warm anyone's heart. We had a shared excitement and enthusiastic curiosity about the spiritual dimension, and I eventually transitioned to partnering with her in this shamanic work. Hanging out on her screened-in back porch or in one of our living rooms felt much more relaxed than a clinical office.

As a seasoned clinical psychologist for the past twenty-five years, Annie was well-versed in both meditation and hypnosis. Partnering with her was helpful as she skillfully guided me to notice my breath and to imagine being surrounded in a protective, healing light. She would count back from ten to one, cueing the tongue-speak to begin. Together, she and I tightened and strengthened the communication system down to a science. We would meet up, step in and out of a metaphysical experience in an hour's time, and then pop back into our normal lives without missing a beat.

Traversing worlds became easily accessible, and the connections felt safe and loving. Yet, I remained dubious. Was this connection legitimate? Were these interpreted messages trustworthy? Open and exploratory, Annie and I enjoyed these interesting adventures together as a unique facet of our friendship. Feeling a curiosity about—and connection with—a magnified power beyond comprehension, we kept coming back to the classroom to hear what I would say.

Understand that your heart is a vast opening, a portal that allows for communication with the soul. There is not a great distance to travel. In fact, there is no distance to travel at all. The unseen is right here. It is superimposed with the physical realm—intermingled with the things you can see, hear, touch, and feel. Both the spiritual and physical realms exist as one continuation, along a vibrational spectrum. There is no separation or duality.

Return to the heart center—the seat of compassion, connection, and love. This energy center in the chest allows you to understand and connect with yourself and others on a deeper level. It is so valuable to get out of your head, your worry, your doubt, and control. Drop to the heart center to experience a sense of love, compassion, and acceptance for your state of being, just as you are.

Practice using the doorway of your heart. This allows your soul to remember. For you, my dear, these practices will help you remember that which you have left behind. Now it is time to practice that which will help you feel more whole. There is no special breath, mantra, or intention. There is nothing to make happen. Drop into the sea of consciousness, of God, of All That Is. Once you are floating there, your only job is to be, absorb, receive, observe—to feel and to know, to remember this was the place before life, and this is the place after life. This is the medicine that heals; this is the knowledge that guides; this is the network that loves, supports, and nurtures the soul. This is the vibration that changes the structure of the mind and how it sees, perceives, and interacts with this world. This is pure Source.

When I was in Catholic elementary schools, I felt a richness and fullness amidst the high ceilings and stain-glassed windows, the sound of prayerful chants, and the smell of incense and old wooden pews. These external cues invited a Godly connection I deeply enjoyed. I found the same to be true in my young adult years of practicing Sikhism. Covering my head, sitting cross-legged on the temple floor, and meditating on the One brought a sense of unity. Yet with mid-life adulthood came a cynical view of all organized religion with its pretenses and hierarchies. So, I retired from religion altogether. I embraced meditation and a relationship with nature to experience a connection with divinity devoid of exterior facades and complicated rules.

However, my husband, Michael—a brilliant, well-patented, well-published metabolic scientist—was evolving in a very different direction. As I traversed beyond the physical here and now into the ethers, Michael ratcheted up his rule-abiding Jewish observance. His nature was rigid, methodical, and disciplined, which is likely why he was so successful in his career. Michael's new and intense attachment to religious disciplines was beautiful to him but quite distressing to my sense of boundless spiritual freedom. When I addressed this discrepancy in our worldviews, it seemed to drive each of us farther into our respective philosophical corners.

Michael wanted to discuss the timing of sunset each Friday night and the ancient laws of the Torah. He became more involved in the Jewish community. I was concerned this layer of religiosity in the home and marriage would interfere with my free-flowing spiritual connection. Though I still couldn't explain or understand it, my strange, new dimension-hopping had become sacred and important to me. It gave me a sense of wholeness, at least, in the fleeting moments when I received channeled information. I hadn't asked for it, but at this point, I was attached to this new relationship with the unknown. I didn't want to lose it.

It does not matter where you live, the time in which you live, or the place where you live; we are here just the same. Rest assured. We will not leave. We are not going anywhere. Trust in that. We will always be right by your side, connected and inseverable until the day you die. Everything, all parts of you, all pieces, all expressions are beautiful and part of your life and your path. You are a whole, dynamic, multilayered, multidimensional being. There is no need to worry, stress, or be afraid.

PRACTICING MEDITATION

While I started most mornings with a few minutes of serene and grounded meditation, my days quickly morphed into back-to-back meetings, rarely allowing me time to breathe, connect, and rebalance. My type A, fiery, bullish, Taurus personality was definitely in the driver's seat, leading the charge towards productivity and achievements.

Recognize that your meditative and spiritual practices allow you to plug in. Like a plug into an outlet, you remember what it feels like to attune to the cosmos—the vibration beyond the self. Self-knowledge and self-awareness are extremely important, yet you are only half of the equation. When you know and understand yourself fully, you realize the other half of the equation is your existence within a much larger environment and a much larger consciousness.

This process of trust and surrender can provide clarity, guidance, support, inspiration, and immense relief from suffering, worry, anxiety, and fear. How do you find this trust? How do you remember there is something so much greater, more intricate, divine, comprehensive, and incomprehensible than the self? This is your homework. This is where you will find the answers. The information available to you is vast, yet you must first practice plugging in. Then, practice frequently. Plug-in, check-in, attune, and align your vibration with the Source of all. This will feel immensely cleansing, grounding, and satisfying. Find clarity, peace, direction, guidance, inspiration, and wholeness. You are completely whole only when the self merges with the non-self. Only then can you move through life with ease and abundance. Expand your consciousness.

Though I had enjoyed a personal meditation practice for many years, it now irritated me that my body trembled each time I sank into a tranquil state. Curiously, the unwelcome convulsions ceased when I consciously allowed the tongue-speak to flow more regularly. Ultimately, by scheduling designated times and spaces to plug in and listen to the guidance offered to me, the uncontrollable shaking and uninvited utterings subsided completely. As long as I created space for this mysterious force to be expressed through me, it somehow honored the boundaries I put in place. Whether these were spiritual guides or something else entirely, we were slowly learning how to exist with one another.

CHAPTER 2

HEALING THE PROTECTIVE LAYERS OF THE HEART

TUNING IN

You are learning that the heart center is an important part of your journey and your practice. Tuning into the heart center is like tuning into a channel on a radio. When you are stuck in judgments and criticisms, it's like listening to static on the radio. Change the channel. You have the ability and the skills to do that. Instead of listening to that static bounce around in your head, consciously drop your energy out of your mind. Breathe. Enter the heart's center of love, compassion, gratitude, and oneness. Suddenly, you are listening to a beautiful symphony, and you notice the delicate nuances that resonate all around you.

Humility and luminescence filled me each time the instructions arrived. Yet, I would often lose the wise clarity just hours after the sessions ended. It was as if a divergent part of my psyche opened during these encounters but was shut off as soon as the visitation ended. I thought to record more of these trance sessions so I could re-listen to them when I was back in my ordinary headspace. I was already in the habit of recording research interviews for my dissertation study, so why not record these sessions, also?

The built-in audio recorder on my iPhone was the simplest solution to capture this off-the-cuff paranormal exploration. This recorder made it especially easy to re-listen to the encounters while I was traveling, working out, or running errands. At first, it was a bit disconcerting to listen to the wise and measured voice that sounded like me but distinctively did not have my personality. How could my voice resonate with such clarity and certainty? How was I guiding myself to live from a wise and loving heart when, in reality, I was a poster child for armored insecurity and detachment? The content being delivered undoubtedly did not originate from my conscious mind.

In addition to audio recording, Annie and I also got into the habit of writing down our questions before I entered the altered state. At this stage of the journey, I was unable to insert my own words or questions when I was deep in the trance. While I was aware of what was happening, and the energy and information channeled through my lips, I was far in the background. Annie and I came up with a system where she read both of our questions out loud after the initial flow of messages slowed down, which allowed space to converse. Our lists inquired about our children, our relationships, and other concerns and curiosities about the details of our lives. Answers followed all of our questions, which often sparked additional teachings. Along the way, we learned of consciousness, ego, and similar topics.

Enter the consciousness of the observer. You notice other people in all of their imperfection. Instead of judging, notice. Even beyond that, instead of just noticing, appreciate, enjoy, and soak up the fullness, magnificence, and unpredictable harmony that exists in this life. Learn to experience from a soul level instead of from a personality level. Personality and ego are necessary protective layers for you to move through this world. As you move through life, you add more layers of protection. All of that is okay. It is part of your design. It is part of the symphony—your uniqueness is part of the whole. But your armor of protective layers becomes a problem when it interferes with your ability to connect with the experience of oneness. As you move through your daily life, notice when your defensive shield interferes with your ability to change the channel and reconnect from the heart.

But be careful, oh spiritual seeker. We are not asking you to live from your pure soul at all times. No! No! No! We celebrate your ability to have a soul connection with the spiritual dimension, but we also celebrate your ability to be in the world—to interact with others, drive a car, and build spreadsheets. These things are not dichotomous. Please understand, accept, and embrace these layers. It is not this or that; it is not black or white, on or off. It is all one. This is the human experience. Learn how to navigate within these different layers and understand how to move in and out as you need to.

Layers indeed. I wrestled with guilt, doubt, judgment, and criticism around this occult practice. Nothing about it felt like a continuum of oneness. I lived in the South, and this was a secret not to be exposed at dinner parties or shared in pre-meeting conference room chatter. As the director of a well-respected clinic, a dedicated wife and mother, and being just months away from holding status with a doctorate, this fractured part of myself didn't fit in anywhere.

My professional circles included psychologists, counselors, and other behavioral health providers. There was no way I was going to invite eyebrows to be raised regarding my mental stability. My limited social circle included my husband's cerebral friends, and I thought it was best to keep this unscientific phenomenon under wraps. "Hi, I'm Siri. I slip into tongue-speak and receive instructions from another dimension." No thanks. Move on, people, nothing to see here. I definitely needed to stay buttoned-up as a normal mother and credentialed health care professional. But dammit, I wished this weird part of me wasn't so palpably soothing and wonderful.

I longed to transcend the painful duality—to breathe easy and live freely and genuinely. It was agony holding this secret. My body was screaming right alongside my pained heart. I had regular headaches, and my low back ached. Several months' worth of Advil and lidocaine patches maintained residence in my dim and messy bathroom closet, and these helpers were also suitcase essentials every time I traveled. I was clearly suffering but wasn't yet ready to admit that to myself.

SOFTENING A WOUNDED HEART

We hear your cries of pain, sadness, and misery when you forget your spiritual connection. In those moments, you forget your soul is always present within you, waiting to awaken. You simply forget where the bridges are, and you forget how to use them. We want you to know how to return when you need to remember the part of yourself that is pure and connected with all. The pathways, doorways, and bridges are always available to you. Surrender, forgiveness, compassion, acceptance, and love are all tools to bridge you back.

Try to understand the layers of the human experience. You are one with the Creator. You are one with creation. At the core, at the soul level, you experience unity. In this oneness, there is no difference between you and another person. You are all part of a stream, as one. Compassion and forgiveness are pathways that can connect your ego with your inner soul. They can serve as reminders that love and unity are at the core, and we are all one with each other. At the soul unity level, forgiveness is not even a concept. There is nothing to forgive because all the actions, interactions, pain, destruction, and perceived separation are all part of the whole. It is all one. These are all part of the actions and reactions of the universe, humanity, and the gestalt of existence. At the personality level, you are separate from the other person. Engaging in forgiveness is important because it reminds you and bridges you back to connecting to the other person in pure love. This is your road map. It is about coming to your core and returning to the soul. Learn where these connectors are—learn where these bridges are that allow you to experience your soul in your daily life.

Great, a road map! If only knowing and doing weren't so impossibly far apart in actual life. Now that I was aware of my wounded and hardened heart, I could more easily spot my patterns of criticizing, shutting down, isolating, pushing others away, and pretending to be happy rather than truly being genuine with my emotions.

My daughters saw right through my hypocrisies, and I knew it. It's always uncomfortable to know others see our flaws and imperfections, but it feels especially humbling to get called out by the next generation. Aren't children only supposed to perceive their parents as gloriously perfect? Kids are so beautifully transparent, and they have an uncanny skill of pinpointing the truth no matter what it's hiding behind. Teenagers do this even more so, and I had one in the house at this point. Teenagers are peering into the abyss of adulthood while still emotionally attuned to the purity of youth. It's like they hold the tension of darkness and light for all of us.

My girls knew I loved them, of course, because I showed my motherly dedication through words, actions, and gifts. I told them I loved them every day; I made them delicious foods, drove them where they needed to go, bought them the supplies required for life, and attended to their daily well-being. Yet my daughters still ragged on my lackluster love. They commented that my version of handholding was a loose, lighter-than-a-feather touch of ambivalence. They called me out for shooing them away when they tried to cozy up next to me in an attempt to cuddle. They couldn't fathom my dislike for domesticated animals or for being woefully non-sentimental. Most of all, they felt the fracture in my marriage and in the home.

Yes, we were fractured. Maybe I wasn't very affectionate. Maybe I even had some intimacy issues. I had no idea what it meant to love myself—I literally had no idea how to do it. And my feelings toward myself (and usually toward others) were often judgmental and critical. Did I really suck at love? Was this why my classroom lessons were so focused on building a heart-centered existence? Maybe I just needed a touch more tenderness, kindness, and compassion. All of this would be easier said than done.

Just a word on love—it is not something you can wait for; it is something you must give because you benefit the most when you love someone else. Yes, you benefit when you receive love. But the most benefit to you comes when you give love.

When you get stuck in judgment and criticism of someone else, your outermost protective layer is interacting with the outermost protective layer of the other person. When you criticize, you remain stuck in the illusion that the outermost layers are all that's there. You must realize that love is so much deeper—its energetic essence reaches deeper than the outermost layers. When you love, the love penetrates to the soul level. Even when you experience self-love, you pierce to your own core. And when you have difficulties with others, if you can love or find compassion or gratitude, you can penetrate past those barriers. You can move past those protective mechanisms and those outermost layers.

Please do not be confused by these teachings. We are not saying you must always live from a place of oneness, pure awareness, and connection. We recognize you must engage your protective layers to survive in the world and navigate within humanity. Trust in yourself and in your soul's journey. Trust that your psyche knows how to protect itself, and trust the unfolding of your path. The outer layer of the ego loves to hold on and control. It's OK. Have patience and trust.

Notice how often you live in your mind. Notice how difficult it is for you to find the heart center and allow it to stay open. Embracing the gentle, loving, compassionate, and trusting energy of the heart brings so much pain as you work through the layers of sadness stored in your core. Move through the sadness as you soften your wounded heart. Soften and settle into more loving energy, or keep your heart center closed and continue to suffer. Your choice is to continue suffering or move through the pain. If you allow yourself to move through the sadness, you can build your resiliency and resolve to live a heart-centered life.

This means living from your heart in all of your relationships, and most of all, it means being honest with yourself. We know this is very difficult for you. This requires courage. Please remember, the way to develop courage is simply to act courageously in small ways every day. You can build your courage over time. It's okay that you are now afraid and do not feel courageous. You recognize your own hypocrisy, your tendency to hide, your pattern of closing down your heart center, isolating, and pushing others away.

Slow down. Move your energy out of your head and into your heart. Open yourself to experiencing new worlds through this soul portal. There will be pain. You cannot live in this world with an open heart and not experience pain. You simply must build the strength and the resiliency to tolerate it. The pain and frustration inside will only get worse if you do not build the tolerance and resiliency to live in wholeness. You must develop robust resiliency to live in your truth.

We know you want more: a life of awe, inspiration, joy, truth, and connection. Remember, we are here and will always be here to support you in your journey. You are never alone. We are always here to guide you to these places you desire. We are here to help you through the pain.

To grow and to meet your authentic self, you must shift your energy and come to your heart center daily. Once you arrive, you can compare the difference between living from your fearful, strategic mind and living from your open, loving heart. You must learn how to balance living from your heart and your head simultaneously. Open mind. Open heart.

I learned not to wear make-up on the days I planned to do this shamanic work because it rubbed off within the first few minutes. Nearly every dimension-traversing session included tears and tissues, even though the deep sense of awe and truth was still present, as well.

These messages were tough to take in. How could I ever climb out of the bottomless well of pain I felt inside? In my waking life, my reality was a million miles away from the wisdom and clarity that spoke through me when channeling. Every time I tried to drop my energy into my heart, all I felt was deep sadness and pain. And I cried a lot of tears.

Practice coming to your heart, tuning into this frequency, and breathing in and out from this point of consciousness. Practice. That is all. Practice living life, making decisions, and being in relationships from this place. It is the only way to build your courage and be consistent. This effort is required to live the life you desire. Start learning from your heart. Choose trust, love, compassion, understanding, sensing, giving, sharing, cooperation, collaboration, peace, fulfillment, satisfaction, contentment, joy, happiness, and patience.

My darling, all the things, qualities, and experiences you desire are right here at your fingertips. Remember, we are partners in this experience of life. We work together, intertwined in every area of your subconscious, your outer world, your dreams, your conversations, your studies, your business decisions, and your discussions. You see, it is all one. It is all the evolution of your own consciousness. You are a part of something so much bigger, so much greater, and your soul is so much more vast than you realize. All of consciousness and all of humankind is more vast than you realize. Trust us through this process—through your growth and your evolution. We are here to serve, guide, and help you. We are here for you to learn from and lean on.

Despite the sadness, the physical sensations of bliss and euphoria during these mystical connections left me with a peaceful wholeness that was the most fulfilling sensation I had ever known. When I was interpreting the cryptic dialect, I felt a calm, grounded clarity. I could not deny that this felt fantastic. It was like I was exactly where I belonged, doing exactly what I was designed to do. I wanted to trust this sense of total oneness, this force beyond comprehension.

After the sessions, though, when I re-inhabited my body and mind, the clarity and wisdom dissolved. Like an addict, I went right back to my life of worry, anxiety, over-controlling, over-achieving, and shutting myself off from my emotions. Doubt crept back in. My faith in fully turning over my trust to a council of invisible guides flickered on and off. Besides, I was busy caring for my tween and adolescent daughters and was barely keeping my stormy marriage afloat. Slowing down to relax into a heart-centered existence was proving to be unbelievably difficult.

Instead, I was now spending more money on clothes, dry cleaning, and jewelry. I was a doctor now and obsessively polishing a pretense of importance to go along with my new credentials. Yet ironically, I was also giving away my power to those whom I regarded as more worthy than myself. Anxiously vying for others' approval, I was eager for my ordination into the realm of acceptance. In short, my protective ego was still calling the shots, and I was attached to the illusion that I'd find security in all the people and places that couldn't actually provide it.

FINDING SECURITY IN THE NON-SELF

Dressed for success, a Venti Starbucks Americano in one hand, a brown leather bag filled with notes for the day's meetings thrown over my shoulder, and an overcrowded keyring jiggling into position in the other hand, my daily race began. What was I racing towards, exactly? Tucked somewhere outside of rational thought, I embraced the fantasy that successful professional achievements would carry me across the finish line, granting magical societal permission to live truthfully, finally incubated against judgment or rejection. I could finally arrive as the true and invincible version of myself with nothing left to prove or to hide. I would finally be free, and I could be honest about my true nature. But like all wonderful fantasies, the imaginary finish line inched farther out on the horizon with each passing day. Arrival was nowhere in sight, just like it hadn't happened after my second marriage, my third academic degree, or my fifth house—each with more promise than the last.

We invite you to consider security, my dear. Security is an important quality for you to contemplate. Where and when are you most secure? When your mind and heart are open and connected, you tap into the vibration of the cosmos. This allows you to experience unshakable trust and security. When you are here, you realize you are part of something indescribably powerful. You can surrender control. You can experience a sense of peace and euphoria. Compare these feelings to the false securities you have attached to in life—the impermanent anchors your mind misinterprets as resolute, such as your job, your clothes, your accomplishments, your connections, and so on. Please realize it is a gross misunderstanding that security can come from these things. These things alone are unmatched to the depth and intricacy of the resolute Source of all creation. When you allow yourself to exist in full acceptance and love of your soul without questioning your security, the universe opens, flows, and provides everything you need as you need it.

I was constantly reading people, trying to figure out what they expected of me, and then delivered that side of myself. This was the case with strangers, colleagues, friends, and even family members. Judgment and criticism flooded me each time I missed the mark. An impenetrable layer of self-doubt separated my decorated costumes and outer masks from the tiny, buried treasure of truth and light deeply hidden within.

I silently projected my own brutal denunciations onto others. When I came across people who displayed bold authenticity and vulnerability—those who didn't care how others perceived them and who were comfortable in their own skin—I wrestled with a mix of criticism, jealously, and inspiration. Could I ever live that openly? Maybe one day. But for now, I had to hold it together, maintain my image, and keep my ego identity safe.

Your lessons, your relationships, and the choices presented to you are all part of your learning—all part of your path, all part of being in this earthly classroom. Let go, surrender, and trust. Do not worry so much about screwing up. If you make choices that do not work for you, you will correct yourself. You will correct, constantly responding to the vibration of the cosmos, constantly tuning-in and checking-in to know how your vibration fits with the world around you. You will receive that feedback. The rest will unfold naturally, and you must trust that unfolding.

Never forget you are a child of this universe. You are never alone. The inspired drives, thoughts, and ideas that move through you—where do you think those come from? You are part of creation. Your vibration, your blueprint, your consciousness in the universe is a unique contribution. When you feel touched or stirred, follow it. Express and manifest. Do not keep it inside.

Attach your sense of security to the non-self, to the Source of all creation. Trust that the flow, knowledge, wisdom, patience, tolerance, joy, connection, inspiration, and guidance will come to you exactly when you need it. Build comfort with us. Surrender. Let go and relax in this process. Practice both getting out of your own way and trusting yourself simultaneously. Find the balance, and the rest will unfold with ease.

As soon as you learn to tap into the universal Source, your life will be so much easier. Surrender. Surrender yourself to the stream of Source energy that exists always and everywhere. This is a true safety net. This is true protection. Nothing can harm you because there is no "you." You are not separate. You see, there is nothing to protect because you are one with all of creation.

— GUIDED —

SLOWING DOWN TO FEEL

Insights and aha moments occurred during long nature walks and hot showers, but rarely when I needed them the most. I needed them amidst the whirlwind that was my waking life. I was so caught up in worldly trappings that I forgot I had access to clear inner wisdom in the moment. Instead, it was as if I got sucked into some kind of vortex, lined with life's illusory demands and expectations.

Practice slowing down, listening, and connecting with the energy that flows through you and the energy in the world around you. Practice noticing the lessons and messages we present to you. Slow down, listen, allow, and notice. It is time to feel the busyness, worry, anxiety, compulsion, and attachment to doing. These are all keeping you from your center and keeping you away from us and your own internal feelings. Your emotions can provide information and messages, and they can provide guidance and clarity about the unfolding and expansion of your consciousness.

You are an entire package, and your feelings inside are, in fact, one of the most important sources of information for how to care for yourself, what your needs are, and what your next step is. Notice these feelings and notice the energy within. This is your work right now. As you awaken, you will open your eyes, open your heart, and open the portal that connects you to us. You must be sensitive, aware, and present, and you must accept and allow whatever comes up. Have the courage to sit within whatever energetic frequency emanates from you.

If sadness arises, know that you can tolerate the sensation. If it is anger, know that you can notice, accept, and tolerate it. Disappointment, fear, whatever it is, we remind you: you have the strength to tolerate it. There is no depth of experience you do not have the capacity to see, accept, and move through. Be not afraid.

I was being given permission to simply be anything and everything that I was. These intense and exciting otherworldly communications had become not only intriguing but special. They were novel and profound, which led me to believe that perhaps I was also novel and profound. This line of thinking misguided me right into the ego trap—I thought maybe I was close to enlightenment. Yeah, not even close.

I would soon slip right back into the comfortably hard shell I had built over the course of my life, holding on tightly, living from the strategic calculations of my protective ego. Why was it so hard to let go, to trust the wisdom of this guidance from beyond? Why was it so hard for me to trust myself? My own heart? My own soul?

We just ask you to slow down enough to feel, notice, be true, and surrender yourself. Get out of your head. Step into the majesty and magic of this world—this extraordinary kingdom that you live within. Connect. Remember. Come back. Return every day. No longer perceive this practice as something that is rare. Return, come back, and remember the extraordinary beauty and possibility of every moment in creation. This is the great unfolding. Return over and over and over again. Return many times per day. Return. Return. Return. There is no place for shame, guilt, or embarrassment in returning. It must be a daily practice. Allow the maintenance of your soul, my love. When you feel a sense of disconnect, getting lost and covered up, that is when you must remember the portal to your soul—the passageway through the heart. You are getting closer. There is so much for you to remember and for you to practice. We are with you. You are not alone. You are never alone.

I learned to appreciate the sensation of surrendering to guidance after taking a beginner's figure skating class with my youngest daughter. The free-floating sensation of gliding across the cold ice hooked me instantly. After graduating from a series of invigorating and humiliating weekend group classes with kiddos in helmets, I signed on for private lessons with a strict Russian coach, whom we will call Konstantin.

HEALING THE PROTECTIVE LAYERS OF THE HEART

Waking up at 4:45 a.m. twice per week to arrive dressed and warmed up on the ice for my 6 a.m. lesson was one of the most disciplined things I had ever done. In time, I fell in love with the dark, early mornings and the big, quiet ice rink. I loved the feeling of cool air tickling my pink face as I stroked up and down the rink. I felt like a superstar sharing the stage with the early morning elite skaters who mesmerized me as they gripped the ice with incredible strength and grace. I soaked up inspiration from these ice angels, knowing I could never perform with even a minute degree of their poise and athleticism.

Ice-skating (or, in other words, balancing on a thin sharp blade) is best learned when being instructed, of course, but also by being held by the coach (both figuratively and literally). I had a strong, exquisitely-composed Russian coach to hold me. Being guided and supported across a risky and slippery surface (much like life) was absolutely formative—a physical and mental practice in surrender and trust. It was scary. It felt uneasy and awkward, but I was safe. Konstantin would not let me fall. This experience taught me to trust, mentally and physically. I learned what it felt like to let go.

CHAPTER 3

OPENING TO CONSCIOUSNESS

ALLOWING THE FLOW

It became a daily practice to transport awareness from head to heart, though it was admittedly more aspirational than successful. I sat on my ragged and worn meditation pillow, trying to imagine the energy from my thoughts, inner dialogue, planning, strategic thinking, and worrying dropping out of my brain, down my throat, and into the center of my chest. I invited spirit and consciousness into my rib cage, aiming to replicate the heavenly state that occurred during the mediated communications. It was tricky because as soon as I thought about it, I was right back into my thinking mind. However, I knew I had arrived when peace and contentment washed over me. Sometimes it only lasted a few seconds; sometimes it lasted several minutes. Either way, it was such a relief to find it. The next step would be to replicate this practice off my meditation pillow out in the world with people, personas, timelines, and egos. Especially egos. Especially my ego.

I was getting to know my heart but still filled with self-criticism, doubt, and embarrassment about my weird occult side. I was still far from authentic, wholehearted living, both with myself and with others.

The uniqueness of your body, mind, and ego are all part of your beautiful blueprint. Work with it, not against it. The energy of all of creation—the energy of the Source—is much like a dance. The exchange of particles, awareness, consciousness, and the learning and expansion of the universe happens in every moment. It is unfolding in a way in which creation learns from itself and grows and interacts with itself. Between two people, there is a bouncing back and forth of energies and concepts—the evolution of each person influenced by the other. And it is as such with all creation. Each individual is only a tiny aspect of the One. Truly, there is no separation. There is only the intellectual concept of the individual human experience.

Recognize that every moment is new and has not yet existed before. And in each moment, you are on the edge of creation itself—of consciousness, of the expansion, and the evolution of the whole universe. Open yourself, open your mind, and open your heart to allow that spark to flow and move through you, outside of your own individual being.

It is imperative to go within to know yourself and work through your blocks and issues. Yet, it can also be a trap to get caught in the mind as a separate individual. You see, every part of your being—of your body, soul, and psyche—has the same Source energy as all other living things. To tap into and open oneself to this realization creates a sense of awe and the opportunity to live in full harmony with others and with all of creation. This is the way of enlightenment. This is the way of spiritual harmony. This is the way of full presence and awareness in every moment.

Allow ideas and opportunities to flow in and out through one mind into the next. Connect with one another in relationships—partnerships, groups, teams, and as a society. Learn how to use the mind to process and condense information. Learn to project and manifest. Yet, be careful, for this is a double-edged sword—the mind can also bind your identity as an isolated self.

This is the trap of the ego. This is where the mind separates you from God and from All That Is.

Most of the time, your energy centers will remain closed in order to function in this world. Yet, there are practices that allow openings: meditation, prayer, being in nature, being in the presence of the great spiritual masters, and shaking up the physical body through dance, exercise, and movements that loosen the constriction of energy and emotion. Also, join communities or groups where the flow of energy is strong (such as prayer groups, worship groups, meditation groups, sharing circles, and other healing circles). It can be easier to access the flow of the Source whenever you have a group of people collectively drawing from that spirit outside of themselves and putting themselves in a state of surrender and receptivity.

Still intrigued and excited about our enigmatic encounters, Annie and I started a small women's circle with other professionals who were also interested in spirituality. We modeled it as a book study group based on the channeled content presented in *A Course in Miracles* by Helen Schucman, though we later expanded into discussing the works of other modern spiritual authors as well.

We met at my home once a month, and I prepared abundant brunches with more artisan chocolate, fresh fruit, baked tofu, homemade biscuits, and similar offerings than our small group could ever eat. It was a joy to make these preparations. It was also a satisfying relief to be with other women who aligned with my intellectual need to question, explore, analyze, and process spirituality and psychic phenomenon.

This intimate professional-spiritual women's group became a safe and sacred place where I could express both parts of myself: my logical, organizational business mind and the newly alive and loving heartfelt side. I had been carrying such deep yearning, such angst and discontent, living with separated selves. It was a much-needed respite to create a small area in my life where I could practice being fully seen and known, honoring all parts of my odd design.

Outside of the once per month gathering, I still bounced between divergent selves. I was a serious, dedicated executive addicted to productivity and married to a successful scientist who worked and produced ten times more than I did. During the weekday hours, nothing thrilled me more than strategizing, analyzing, and building a beautiful spreadsheet, telling an unequivocal story of success. Yet on the weekends, each time I pierced the veil, I felt a calm, wise, and clear energy. My body's tightly jumbled knots of tension disappeared. I floated in absolute freedom, love, and ecstasy as soon as the utterings began. As each visitation ended, I felt heavy and achy. After just a few hours, I got used to the discomfort of inhabiting my body all over again, forgetting I had ever escaped it at all for a brief period. I went right back to living in my head, planning, and fantasizing about the future.

Regarding your concerns about your future: stay calm and trust. Return to the heart, to the portal in the center of the upper chest. Remember that experiencing energy from this place is a gateway into another dimension—a place that allows you to see and experience the self and the world with greater wisdom and compassion. This is also the place of trust; knowing and remembering your life path is unfolding just as it should. Return to the heart to love, to trust yourself, and to trust the divinity and intricacy of All That Is. So often, you get worried and anxious about the unfolding of your path, your future, and living your full potential. It's a waste of energy to worry like this. When you add the anxiety of worry, when you pray so fervently for your future, you are only creating blocks that detract you from living in your full alignment and potential in the moment. Stay present.

Trust your path. Enjoy and take pleasure in it. You are evolving, and your life is unfolding exactly as intended. The pressure you put on yourself is unnecessary. Not only is it unnecessary, it actually burdens you. This heaviness takes you away from the clear consciousness of living in the states of joy and love. The magic happens when you return to the heart. This is where you can live in awe and gratitude, fully experiencing the pleasure of being in this life.

HAVING FUN ALONG THE WAY

As an exhausted mother tiptoeing in a fragile home environment, I wasn't having much fun. But to be honest, I didn't even know what fun looked like for me. I was jealous of people who packed up the kids and went on camping trips, had fire pits, and parties in their backyards, or owned boats and spent as much time on the lake as they did at work. But that wasn't my family—we were the serious, over-planning type. Recreation wasn't in our vocabulary. Ice skating was the first hobby I ever picked up as an adult, and that was more about discipline than play. This spiritual growth journey was proving to require quite a bit of discipline, as well.

I entertained the idea that maybe God touched me with a unique spiritual gift to share with the world, but this idea added even more pressure. I didn't feel worthy of being the arbiter of such a gift. Filled with fear and cowardice, I had denied this part of myself for so many years, and I still wasn't fully honoring it.

Be very true to your own vision and inner knowing. Connect deep within. Settle into yourself and move through your world more slowly and gently, both with yourself and with others. Be purposeful, intentional, and clear. Observe every moment. Recognize what your experience is. Get curious and challenge movement in your thoughts, emotions, or energy. Experience that moment from a different place. Understand your ability to move through different mental and emotional states and different vibrational frequencies. Observe, slow down, and listen.

And have fun! Don't take yourself so seriously. There is always the opportunity to experience joy and have fun with this process of life. It does not have to be so serious. This practice of incorporating joy will serve you, enhance your work, your relationships, and your personal sense of contentment and peace. When your energy becomes heavy, you miss so much. You stay so busy, so covered up with the attempt to stay safe and secure, but instead, you remain distant. Just listen. Feel. Sense deeply. We are with you, and you are safe. If you can surrender and allow it, it will not be so painful. It does not need to be painful. Simply allow your being to be born into itself and its purpose.

— OPENING TO CONSCIOUSNESS —

You always have a choice in whether you accept or deny your soul's journey. You have free will, and it is up to you to align with your soul or to stay hidden. We will be with you no matter what choices you make. We will never leave your side. We were placed with you in this life and will be with you forever. You must understand you did not design this. We were chosen as your team, as your support, and as your guides. We are with you. We are in this together, and nothing will ever change that.

It is okay to surrender. You do not have to fight it. It is okay to accept this. In your acceptance, you will find the happiness you seek and the peace of walking your path with certainty. No more hiding. No more covering up or pretending. Step in. Simply allow what is to be. That is all you have to do right now. In fact, there is no doing. In life, you have done enough. You have worn yourself thin. You have worn yourself out. There is no need to push, to prove, or to do. Now simply listen and allow. Let it be. You will hear our messages every day. We are not going anywhere. You will not be alone.

This idea of having fun was invigorating. It was just the permission I needed to unwind and reconnect with my free-spirited, playful side. I looked around and noticed the people who moved through life with pleasure and enjoyment. My kids urged me to lighten up and play. My dad inspired me to pull out my bike and take a spin every now and again. A friend invited me onto her boat, and I actually said "yes." Several times! This was feeling good, and I wanted more of it.

LISTENING TO THE BODY

I had a knot the size of Texas in my right shoulder, and each massage therapist I visited suggested weekly bodywork to ease the built-up tension. I was still holding my body in a perpetual state of defense, anxiously on guard to protect my most sacred asset: the delicate, beautiful, divinely-connected soul within. It would still take a few more years for me to realize I could protect my sacred spirit through words and actions, rather than tensing up my muscles and wearing psychologically-protective armor all the time.

The portal of the heart center is a doorway. When you can drop your energy into the heart, into the center of the chest, there you will find a portal—a trapdoor into another reality. This reality cannot be seen with the naked eye and cannot be felt with the hands or the feet of the body. You can only sense and recognize it through vibrational frequency—through its emotional overtone. For how do you know when you are happy, at peace, or in euphoria? You know these states because of the physical sensation the emotions produce in your body. You know because you feel the sensations in this area, this portal, this doorway within the torso.

Next, to work with energy, you must nurture your sensitivity and awareness. Refine your attunement to understand the invisible properties of energy. Understand what constricted energy feels like and what you sense when energy beyond you flows through you. This practice requires physical awareness. Understand the impact your energy and emotions have on your breathing, heart rate, muscular tension, ease of communication, and flow in your life. Refine your understanding of what it means to be in the flow. Feel the rhythm of flow, and feel the rhythm of constriction. Recognize the physical and emotional signs. Know and understand the practices that stimulate the opening and closing of energy centers in the body.

I understood how the nervous system reacted to both trauma and healing through my work in eating disorders and my study of mind-body medicine. I poured over several thick research publications on the neurobiology of emotional healing to deliver a handful of presentations on the topic. Remembering the earlier experiences of my body's shaking and convulsions, the wisdom of the nervous system and its role as communicator struck me. There is an alignment of the nervous system and the psyche. This connection is present not only in the healing of trauma but also in the evolution of consciousness and spirituality.

I tried to bring awareness to the various physical states of my body. I noticed how it responded to feelings of emotional safety (relaxed and grounded) versus the feelings of insecurity or anxiety (buzzing, constricted tension coursing through me). When I visited massage therapists while traveling and they asked what kind of work I wanted to be done, I responded, "Just remind my body to relax. Remind my body that it's safe and OK to let go."

ENGAGING THE INTELLECT

Since intertwining thoughts and emotions manifest physically in the body, the intellectual-psychological work was just as important (if not more important) than the physical bodywork. I became curious about self-observation, including my patterns of thought, behaviors, and decision-making. Most of all, I was ready to address the fact I was still hiding from the most sacred part of myself.

We want to teach you to see through. Not to see what is on the surface, but to see through any situation, person, event, opportunity, or task—to make unclouded decisions. This does not detract from engaging your cognitive mind, gathering information, and making appropriate decisions. Understand that both are necessary. Do not become mentally lazy. We are not guiding you only to feel and not to think. Please do not misunderstand. Engaging your intellect will always be important. Instead, expand the breadth of ways you take in information and make decisions. Do not place more weight on intellect and less on intuition. The opposite also applies: do not place too much weight on your own intuition and miss the intellectual exercises of disciplined thought. Both can be flawed.

Remember to operate from love, patience, and clear intentions. Your meditation practice will help you identify the areas requiring resolution, guidance, and closure. When you continue to get lost, spinning in thoughts, worry, concern, overwhelm, frustration, stress, and tension, let it all go. Return to the portal, which allows you to plug into Source energy, where everything unfolds in harmony with great ease and without your control. Trust. Trust. The most important guiding principle for you is trust. There is no need to doubt yourself. There is no need to worry. All you have to do is trust the process. Just trust yourself, trust us, and trust that you sit in the middle of a vast universe which supports you and all the elements of its creation. You are not isolated. You are not separate. You are supported.

Trust. Operate from love. Be clear in your intention. Continue your meditation practice. You will be fine, and we are here. We are not going anywhere. You can come to us anytime.

Rationally, I was still asking basic questions. Where exactly was this energy and information coming from, and who exactly was "us"? Was I ready to believe these to be the voices of spiritual guides, ascended masters, and guardian angels? Was I able to fully surrender and trust this dimension beyond my comprehension?

This sage advice had never led me astray over these past many years. On the contrary, these communications guided both the interior and exterior of my life in gentle and profoundly healing ways. There was no doubt a sincere psychic-spiritual connection was occurring—one that was genuine and trustworthy. So, yes. At this point, I was finally ready to surrender to, believe in, and trust this guidance from beyond.

CHAPTER 4

SHIFTING DISCONNECTION TO INTERCONNECTION

SURRENDERING TO THE GREAT PARTNERSHIP

For years now, I had been a faithful believer in the unfathomable power (and limitations) of the mind. I was proud of the black and white bumper sticker clinging to my Subaru Outback that read, "Don't believe everything you think," as an invitation for fellow drivers to move beyond limiting thoughts and small-minded interpretations of reality. I remained single-mindedly focused on achieving my professional, financial, and personal goals in life. I loved journaling, vision boarding, and intention-setting, though I often gave myself headaches from overthinking and future-projecting. (Luckily, I still had an abundance of Advil on hand.) Isolated in my own fantasies, I falsely believed my projections alone held the power to construct any destiny I imagined.

Intention setting has value, so please continue to use your mind and your meditation to attain clarity and set your intentions. Write it. Repeat it. Remind yourself so your actions and behaviors match your mindset. This practice is good and fruitful. Yet when you reach the point of casting off your intentions into the universe, you must let it all go. Surrender completely. Continuing, continuing, and continuing to pray, worry, and mentally project becomes too much of a burden on your psyche, which interferes with your ability to manifest.

You understand the basic process of using your thoughts to manifest your reality. Set your intention and align your actions daily. Beyond that, you must let go. Trust and know we are working just as hard as you are. We are working in another realm, in the spiritual dimension, while you are working in the mental and physical dimensions. You are using your mind to project, which affects your energetic frequency. You are making decisions and taking actions that match your desires. Adding prayer through your partnership with us means you are working in the spiritual realm, as well. We are working just as diligently. Please trust that everything is in motion.

So much that happens is beyond your comprehension, beyond your ability to see. In all things, and for all people, this is true. You are not unique in this. Everyone has guides and angels around them. You will soon learn more about how the universe opens up to serve you when you remain dedicated to serving it. This is the great partnership.

To worry, anxiously pray, and repeat your intentions and concerns over and over shows a lack of trust and understanding in us and our part of things. You do not need to micromanage us. You can ask once. Set your intention, set forth your prayer, let it go, and trust. When you release control over the outcome, things always manifest with far more sophistication than anything you could conjure on your own. There is so much more happening beyond your ability to comprehend. You must trust that this is where we work. You will not always receive everything you wish for, yet we hope you will begin to see how we are working on your behalf towards your conscious evolution.

Sometimes, when I was bored with whatever podcast or audiobook I was listening to, I would re-listen to the audio recordings of these transcendent teachings. While I drove to and from work, hopped on the treadmill at the gym, and walked through airports, I listened to my own voice deliver wise and soulful instructions in broken tongue-speak and English. It was both odd and wonderful, concerning and comforting. Once I got past the strangeness of the recordings, these private study sessions anchored the lessons. They also secured the reality that I lived in two worlds, with a foot in each one. When I heard my voice in this way, it became harder to ignore and push aside my shamanic identity.

All things are in motion. We invite you to bring us into your life daily. When you come to the portal of the heart, you can bring more love, compassion, wisdom, creativity, connection, and understanding into all you do and see, including the decisions you make and how you communicate. We would like to help you manifest your intentions. Let us help you at every level. We always will and always have been with you, whether you realize it or not. We are working behind the scenes constantly, yet when you accept and open to us, you amplify our efficiency. This partnership allows you greater alignment in your life.

Your soul's portal is always here, always accessible, and always open. We are here, however, and whenever you need us. This connection requires a surrender of your ego. It requires a rearranging of your psyche and of all the personality veils and illusions you have developed over the course of your lifetime to feel a sense of safety and protection. Understand these layers are only illusions. They do not protect your soul. In fact, they do the opposite. These layers keep you from connecting deeply and strongly with the Creator. They are your mind's way of trying to keep yourself safe. Yet your soul is indestructible—it can neither be created nor destroyed in this life. You have a built-in lifeline within. The portal through your heart is your internal communication device. This pathway is your soul's instant connection back to us, back to God, and back to the very place where all souls reside. The portal within you is a direct connection to the vibration of all of creation.

Annie and I spent hours dissecting what happened in the classroom sessions. We discussed the content of the messages as well as the visions and symbolic imagery that merged in my consciousness alongside the words being spoken. We marveled at the physical sense of bliss and awe during the encounters, and while Annie wasn't feeling in her body what was moving through mine, she reported clear and distinct changes in my facial expressions, tone of voice, and body language, all indicating a significant energy shift was occurring.

We began digging into writings of other spiritual channels and realized that these mystical-psychic phenomena were not unique to us. Annie and I shared stories of how the guidance touched and affected our daily lives. The profundity of it was undeniable, and it was getting harder to dismiss the validity of these reproducible encounters.

As I grappled with the idea of acceptance, my external life continued to unfold. I was promoted to a C-level executive position with more responsibilities overseeing a network of eating disorder and substance abuse treatment programs. I pivoted into big picture systems, data analysis, and complex budgets. My new professional identity strengthened my ego's resistance to embracing my enigmatic side.

GETTING OUT OF THE WAY

It is important to get out of your own way and let the flow of creation happen through you. Dance with it, be one with it, and understand it is running through you. You can allow it, push it away, hold on to it tightly, or continue to support the

SHIFTING DISCONNECTION TO INTERCONNECTION

flow. You can maintain a sense of control of your own energy, staying closed off from the larger creation, or you can see God and spirit as interweaving within and outside of you, simultaneously. Allow yourself to be a co-creator with the Source energy. Allow it to move through you. Choose it. Accept it. Dance with it. Bring in your own personality, your unique soul print. Mix and mingle. Gently allow the humility and confidence as both student and colleague of creation.

I wasn't quite out of my own way yet, though I was learning to accept more of the energies and emotions that moved through me. The sadness became more tolerable. In fact, I somehow found compassion for the sadness over time. After all, I was the one who had pushed my truth so deeply out of reach. There was no one else to blame, although it took me a few years to come to this conclusion after trying to blame everything on my husband. No, I was the one who had buried my heart. Maybe I thought it was the only way to protect my sacred and sensitive nature, but I can't be sure because I don't even remember when or how this happened. Surely, I never intended to disown or fragment such a core part of my soul or psyche. Maybe my heart was healing. Maybe consciousness was emerging. Maybe I was more connected with God.

Know that inspiration and awareness can come directly into the mind in moments of silence, meditation, or contemplation. We have access to feed you, guide you, and inspire you—that is our job. That is exactly what we are here for. Please, please use us as often as you can because we are here to serve. We are here to help. We are here to support your life, to make things easier and clearer, to help you understand, and to help clarify these things that confuse you. Ask. Open the dialogue. It is okay to question. Allow yourself to be open and to receive. Get out of your own way. Get out of your old constrained thinking so you can truly receive, truly hear the guidance we are offering you. Then, the answers we are giving you will finally become known. It is all available to you at every moment. The answers are already swirling around you. Surrender. Cease your over-thinking. Let that go. Surrender and open yourself up to the consciousness that resonates in all of creation.

UNLOCKING THE PSYCHE

One night, I dreamt I was walking along a dirt path deep in the woods. I came upon an old, white cottage. It was comfortable and familiar. I stepped onto the simple stone back porch steps, opened the rickety screen door, and entered the home. An aging man of Asian descent was sweeping the wooden floor. He looked at me with a loving smile, as though he had been expecting me. The tall, lean man quietly handed me the broom, gesturing it was my turn to sweep the floor. He then walked out of the rickety screen door, letting it bounce against the wooden frame as it closed. The words "Tao Te Ching" reverberated, a pronouncement. I had no idea what this meant, but it felt so memorable I thought maybe this was a visitation from a man named Tao Te Ching. I didn't even know how to spell these words, so it took a few minutes to figure it out, with the help of Google.

To my surprise, I didn't find a man with this name, but an ancient Chinese text called *Tao Te Ching: The Book of the Way* by Lao Tzu. This was a book about Taoism, which I knew nothing about. I ordered the book on Amazon and felt a flutter of excitement when it arrived. The slim and simple book sat on my office side table for months. Somehow, it brought me comfort just having it sit nearby. I sometimes thumbed through it, finding guidance during hectic days and tough decisions. Through this book, I was introduced to the path of slow, gentle wisdom.

Lessons were now showing up in places where I least expected. Information and insights were everywhere: in the trance sessions, in my dreams, and in my waking life. I

— GUIDED —

felt more connected with a sense of self-awareness and also interconnected with something outside of myself. Not just in the otherworldly classroom sessions but also in more ordinary moments.

The mind is a powerful tool for practicing imagery and visualization. See your body's energy systems like wires and vessels. Imagine and connect with the flow of energy. See it moving. Imagine the blockages and experience how much the mind influences your energy.

Use the mind to decide whether or not to practice compassion. Then use your mind to notice the energy state of your body when you are compassionate. If you decide to practice criticism, use the mind to notice the sensation in your body when you are critical. The mind holds a great deal of leverage and command in how you experience life. It is a powerful machine, much like a train conductor pulling a lever to open or close tracks for where the train should go. An important function of the mind is to choose which direction your energy flows.

Remember, you do not need to analyze to know the flow that is alive in all of creation. Tapping into this energy is far simpler than you imagine. Open, receive, and allow the flow to move through you. Open the doorway at the third eye and the crown chakra to allow direct access to intuition and universal wisdom.

— SHIFTING DISCONNECTION TO INTERCONNECTION —

The mind is another portal, another doorway. When the chatter and static of the mind lift and one experiences an inspirational flow of thoughts, ideas, and creativity from beyond the self, where do you think it comes from? It is not from you. It is not from your intellect, nor your cunning thought. The portal of the mind can serve as another gateway of truth.

CONNECTING WITH TRUTH

I loved both my job and my kids with great passion. The only problem was I didn't love myself yet. I didn't honor myself yet. I was still hiding and spending far too much energy keeping up the facade of being a normal Southern wife, mother, and professional. It nauseated me. Literally. I had developed an ulcer, so I picked up some Omeprazole at the store, which helped a little.

I was adept at putting everyone else's needs before my own. I moved through my days with an agreeable grin plastered on my face until no one was looking. Drinking a few glasses of red wine, a bourbon cocktail (usually with a cherry), or a vodka and juice combination (also with a cherry) had become my evening ritual. Once I was comfortably numb, I grabbed some chocolate or other yumminess and spaced out in front of a ridiculous Netflix drama to escape. Getting as far away from myself as possible was just the relief I needed to release the pent-up tension of always pretending to be someone other than exactly who (and what) I was.

My darling, it is time for you to work from the spirit, from the heart. You are so busy working in the material world. Now it is time for you to do the internal work. It is time to breathe, flow, and dance in an integrated way, not living in separate worlds with a gap of numbness in the middle. You are ready to open your eyes. You are ready to live in truth. It is time to exercise your heart, to feel its connections and pulsations.

As you hide in pain and misery, a shadow of darkness is vibrating out into the world, affecting you and those around you. Become aware of your own beating heart, the portal of your soul, and your unique blueprint. Accepting it changes your energy and the energy you send out into the world. There is no shame and embarrassment in your blueprint. Allow it to be. You are holding it back—scared, hiding, avoiding, and shutting it off. Allow what already is. Unplug what you have stopped up. When you shut down, it is harder to hear and follow our messages.

Please open your heart and your eyes. You have only one heart and one spirit. Honor your truth. Hold your truth above all else. Truth is not a belief or thought. Truth is simply existing with what is. Allow your spirit to vibrate at its own frequency. There is nothing to do but allow and accept.

I was deeply ashamed of my hypocrisy. I held a doctorate in mind-body medicine and espoused healthy stress management techniques. My early career was built on the principles of meditation, nutrition, and self-awareness, and for the last several years, I led teams of psychologists, therapists, nutritionists, yoga instructors, and other healing professionals in guiding patients towards recovery from eating disorders and addiction.

I was a hypocrite and a coward. I knew what to do, but I wasn't putting that knowledge into action. It felt too hard to take that next step—to come to terms with the hidden occult part of myself I didn't understand, couldn't explain, and didn't know how to fit into my life. It was time to get courageous and move out of my misery, but the thought of coming out felt insurmountable. Nope. Not now. Maybe not ever. I remained isolated, embarrassed, depressed, and stuck.

Fear and isolation come when you separate yourself from creation, sever the connections with the All That Is, and stay attached to your own fantasies and outcomes. This is isolation of the ego. This is when you experience frustration and disconnection.

Build trust with God, Creator, guides, and the spiritual realm. Develop and build trust with your own spark within—your own connection with divinity. Understand where it lives and what ignites it. Know what it feels like to ignite and to feel alive. Take note. Be as descriptive as you can in understanding the feeling, sensation, and experience of being spiritually connected—of being in the flow. Identify which practices, decisions, and actions helped you to settle into flow and connection. Take note so you can replicate these practices, decisions, and actions to bring you closer to peace, joy, fulfillment, and the gates of heaven.

Be with us. Experience harmony. Experience oneness. Experience being. Take note. Understand how to get here and begin developing your own road map. Know the road so you can choose to take it whenever you like. But remember, there is more than one path. There is more than one road. Map all of them so you can travel, so you can arrive at the experience you desire, so you can feel relief from the anxiety, separation, and isolation. Map the way for yourself. It may be different from someone else's path. It doesn't matter.

The kingdom of heaven (symbolically and metaphorically) is available to you, lives within you, and is something you can tap into throughout your life before you die. Feel the connection with divinity—it is available to you. Even when you feel

SHIFTING DISCONNECTION TO INTERCONNECTION

the slightest glimpse of peace, map it out. Likewise, when you feel isolation, anxiety, frustration, and depression, understand what got you there. Understand the practices, decisions, and experiences along the path that landed you at the destination of misery and suffering.

You will experience pain and joy throughout your life in ways that are beyond your control. These are not the things we are referring to. We are only referring to the patterns of your mind—your behaviors and choices that create a life that can be miserable or enjoyable. Notice your frame of mind, your connection or disconnection to that which is greater than yourself.

After several more months of silent suffering, I finally found the bravery to let go, to feel. I knew I had to stop drinking alcohol. That would be the first step, but it would still take six months for me to execute that genius plan. Then, I would need to rebalance my relationship with food and limit my evening screen time. Without numbing out, all that would remain would be my uncomfortable emotions, my trembling ego, and the awkward truth of who I was. As scary as those realities were, I no longer had a choice. I hated living in cowardly hypocrisy. It was miserable. It was time to accept the sadness of my wounded heart, courageously feel my emotions, and be true to myself.

We understand what you are going through. You are brave and courageous to allow your emotions to emerge. They will pass. Emotions are just messages, and first, you must heed their message. They are not something to be afraid of. They are not something to run away from or to cover up. They are a message from your spirit. Have the courage to do what you need to do. Your destiny is not sadness forever. You are safe. You are free. You are a child of the universe, and everything you need is at your disposal. Relax. Listen to the voice inside and what it says now. Trust in what emerges. We are here to guide, nudge, and support you in the subtle realm where we communicate with you. Instead of remaining tied up in the busyness of your life, we ask that you notice and trust the subtle guidance we provide for you. That is all. It is that simple. It only requires you to listen and respond. Trust your senses, drives, instincts, and intuitions.

It felt invigorating to honor the emotions inside my chest. But it was also tough to do so without a numbing agent on hand. There were so many things I didn't want to feel and so many situations I didn't want to face. Maybe using alcohol wasn't really a problem. Maybe it was just the bottled gift I needed, after all.

But no, I wanted to feel strong. I wanted to feel brave. I wanted to give myself the gift of honesty. Other people

SHIFTING DISCONNECTION TO INTERCONNECTION

could do it. I had witnessed—and even guided—countless individuals and families along the raw and exhilarating path of recovery from brokenness to healing, from lying to truth, from hiding to being seen. If they could all do it, then surely, I could do it, too.

Open yourself to connect with the lightness of being, allowing this light to flow all the way through the body to awaken your health and vibrancy. But do not let it in just to hold it selfishly within the body. Recognize that your own fears and insecurities block the flow. You limit the flow when you attempt to control it. Understand there is a difference between energy moving within the closed circuit of the body and energy moving through the body—breathing, connecting, and dancing with all of creation.

Once you learn how to use your mind, you must realize its limits. Directly plugging into the Source can occur without cognition. Bathing in the light and energy of the stream of consciousness can occur outside of the mind. This experience of pure connection is like bathing in healing light.

Over time, the sharp lines of duality between my two selves softened around the edges. In small and subtle ways, peaceful and gentle guidance emerged into my conscious mind as I navigated daily conversations and decision-making. Transparency felt more natural than hiding, and my mothering, marriage, and leadership style reflected this shift. The rhythm of my intuition was gently tapping inside. I noticed tugs, cries, and invitations emanating from my heart. I didn't always listen to them, but I had a glimpse of where they came from and how I might access a connection with that part of myself, should I desire to do so.

CHAPTER 5

AWAKENING THE INDESTRUCTIBLE SOUL

COMING OUT OF HIDING

I drove the seven long hours across Tennessee to arrive in my hometown of Memphis. Upon arriving in the early afternoon, I connected with my mom and dad. After salads and sandwiches at Panera, we went to the movie theater for the debut of *Rocketman*. I sobbed through the life story of Elton John. He lived in pain for years before accepting and loving his wounded heart, yet he boldly expressed his distinct uniqueness all along the way. The depth of emotion swelled my heart, and the fractures in my protective armor gave way.

The next morning, my heart burst, no longer able to carry the burden. That humid summer morning, still wearing my salmon-colored satin nightgown with no make-up and my hair tied in a bun, I sat with my parents on their patio and cried like a baby. I explained I could no longer exist in hiding, but I simply didn't know how to move forward carrying my secret. I think my parents were equally relieved and dumbfounded when I exposed my hidden spiritual gift, rather than something spicier like illegal drug use, homosexuality, or a clandestine love affair.

Nonetheless, my conservative Christian parents gave me a priceless gift that day. They held a non-judgmental space big enough to contain my dripping sorrow. They accepted and honored me, recognizing I had always been a little different. Their unconditional acceptance bolstered my courage and fed my confidence to move forward in embracing my own unique truth.

I am a tongue-speaker who perceives energy and information from a nonphysical dimension. I am guided by a force beyond comprehension, and I communicate with departed souls from time to time. I shared the whole truth with Michael, who had always known, even though I rarely talked about it. I openly expressed my total self to both my teenage and young adult daughter, who, like my husband, admitted this was no surprise. Apparently, the strange sounds of another language don't blend in with the daily noises of a bustling home, as the melodies of my unique heart song had been commonplace over the years.

I told a few friends. I expressed my truth in a few meaningful professional relationships, and I was relieved to be met with support. All the way around, it was an enormous blessing to receive acceptance outside of my small, safe women's circle. I was aware that some who courageously step into their genuineness are met with condemnation and hatred, and this was my concern all along. I was immeasurably grateful for how my coming-out experience transpired. It felt amazing and immensely freeing to express the full integrity of my spirit to the people in my life who meant the most to me. However, coming out to the rest of the world would be a slower, more bashful process.

We welcome your eyes to open, your heart to open—your path and your life to open. You are like a small child beginning to open her eyes. Do not worry about the next steps. Remember, this process is like a radio tuner. Be clear and go inside, towards your center. It is like turning a dial. When you get to that place where the heart sings, and the peace sits within you, stay there. Explore your different channels, and when you get tuned in to the place where your soul resides, stay there, listen, feel, and let it vibrate through your whole being—through your body, your mind, your ego, and your aura. Allow yourself the time to play and explore. Remember who you are. Explore who you are. The song of your heart you have been working so hard to protect and hide no longer requires hiding and protecting. It is safe to come out now. You are safe.

Your soul is always safe and can never be harmed. It is only the personality and the ego (the outer layers) that can be damaged. The soul cannot be destroyed. You can choose to stay asleep because, somehow, it feels safer to keep the soul hidden. No more. Lead with the soul. You have awakened. Honor the beauty of your soul with all your heart and mind.

I promised myself I wouldn't hide anymore. I attempted to move through my days and evenings more slowly, consciously, and honestly. I aspired to remain present and aware even on the messiest, most awkward of days. And like every other step of this spiritual journey, it was far easier said than done. I still fretted about the future. I worried about coming out fully and building my life more authentically.

The world you have created for yourself is ready for you, and you are ready to express yourself into the world. Too often, you let the world around you dictate how to behave, what to say, what to wear. Too often, the choices and decisions you make are because of others, not because you are vibrating in full integrity with the frequency of your soul. Know your own spirit, your essence, and what you bring to this world. That is when you are at peace. Remember, you are complete, just the way you are. We realize it is not easy to live in this world as you are, in the full integrity of your soul.

Remember, it is like tuning the dial on a radio. You get static, and you cannot quite make out who you are anymore. You cannot quite make out the sound of your own voice. You know it is there, but you can't quite get to it. It's not coming in clearly. For you, the practice is to find your heart station. Stay there and allow the signal strength to get stronger and clearer. The more clearly you resonate at the frequency of your soul, the easier it is to tune back in, and the easier it becomes to listen to its wisdom. It is a practice—a practice of listening, allowing, honoring, and loving yourself. Love the frequency of your soul. Trust the divine Source within your soul because that spark connects to

God in everything and all of creation. Your unique spirit is part of the beauty of creation. It is time to trust that. Allow yourself to live in the integrity of your soul. No more hiding. You have been hiding long enough.

Allow yourself to be a doorway, as we have created you to be. You will serve as a gateway between these worlds, going in both directions. For you to function in alignment with your purpose, you must understand that this is your design. The practice and discipline of humility are necessary to continue with this work and way of being. If you, your ego, and your mind get in the way of the connection, you will suffer and struggle. Your humility is what keeps you open to us. It is what will keep you fulfilled, content, and serving your purpose in this life.

Know, accept, and embrace the connection to the power you have access to and to the path we are helping you see. You can then use the rest of your life to fulfill your design and to experience deep happiness, joy, and fulfillment. It is that simple. Nothing is complicated here. It is time to accept and trust.

I spoke honestly about my gifts when casual conversations with acquaintances allowed for it. This opened the doors for several channeling sessions with friends and family members. I learned how to enter and exit the otherworldly trance state on my own long ago, so I was able to offer this unique experience of spiritual connection without Annie by my side. I traversed worlds while sitting outside on a blanket in my front yard with a neighbor, while settled in a wicker rocking chair at my parents' home, and while sitting on my brown leather living room couch with a friend. Additional similar encounters with others fortified my trust and belief in this unexplained phenomenon. I was coming to peace with the fact that I was somehow designed to live with access to not just one but two dimensions.

You have a beautiful, beautiful gift to share with the world. Simply allow and listen. Be not afraid. Relax into it. A new life is beginning for you. Allow the birth to take place. Take joy in the beauty of this creation. Allow yourself to enjoy, to embrace. You do not need to hide your joy any longer. You are safe to be what you are—to embrace, love, and enjoy. Do not be shy. Do not be afraid. We are here with you. Do not be afraid to know and understand the portal the Creator has built within you.

CHOOSING JOY AND LOVE

I was consciously trying to follow the instructions given to me and was growing weary of feeling negative and resentful so much of the time. As my colleagues and friends in recovery would say, I was sick and tired of feeling sick and tired. I was still harboring significant doubt, fear, anger, criticism, and judgment directed towards myself and others, and I wanted to recover more quickly after getting emotionally activated by these states. I felt angst and restlessness, now having a glimpse of what was missing: the embodied experiences of emotional safety, contentment, and love within myself and within my relationships with other people. True to my intense, over-achieving nature, I put too much pressure on myself to make these major recalibrations.

At the soul level, you are rearranging the bricks in the wall. Imagine the wall as representative of your inner foundation and your outward identity. Allow yourself to construct and rebuild with steadiness, peace, and ease. Let the light of your soul guide you and relax into this process. Truly, there is no need to bring stress, tension, and worry during the rebuilding process. In fact, this is a beautiful and joyous process to be celebrated.

The amount of passion and emotion and, ultimately, the amount of energy you put into things fuels what you do. Yet, please understand you can separate the intensities and types of energy. Separate passion and emotion from stress, tension, worry, and anxiety. The tension, anxiety, and worry only interfere. It does not fuel your progress. It hinders it. The things that fuel spiritual progress and flow into all aspects of your life include joy, being relaxed, and operating from your heart with a sense of trust. Trust in the universe, and trust that you are part of that trusted Source. Trust that when you can perceive life with joy and lightness, your ideas, creations, relationships, and opportunities will propel forward with inspiration and love. You are now understanding. Allow yourself to experience these states. Relax. Enjoy.

You want to learn to concentrate, to focus. These are critically important, but focusing too strongly can create rigidity, tension, worry, and anxiety. You have gone over the edge with these energies in an attempt to manifest exactly what you desire, and this is interfering with your easy sync with the universal energies. Remember to do the things that bring you to a state of joy, relaxation, and flow in your mind, in your heart, and also in your body. Playful movement with children, enjoyable exercise, joyful dance, hiking in nature, rejuvenating yoga—these activities can diffuse the energy, shake off the tension and static, and allow you to settle into that state of clarity and focus.

Connecting with the world, plugging in, and receiving support allows an exchange of energy that puts you in the flow. This flow moves through all the energy centers of your physical body. My dear, you must learn to think, know, and receive from your entire self, from your entire body, from your total energy—not just through your mind. It is a misunderstanding that all of your awareness happens in your mind. There are gateways throughout your entire body that both send and receive energy and information. There is so, so, so much more to experience in this world than just your limited cognitive experience. Open yourself up to give and receive.

Focus on relaxing your energy, including your physical body, so that consciousness can move through you with ease. Stay relaxed to allow joy and flow. This is a wonderful exercise to help you identify what interferes with your process of establishing joy as a value and a conscious decision in your life. You have blocked joy. It is low on your list of priorities. Look at your thoughts and values, and notice what interferes with your ability to experience joy, relaxation, rejuvenation, and wholeness. It is time to inspect the elements that take up your time and energy but are not working for you. We will help you in this process of identification and clarity. We will help you re-prioritize. We will guide you.

You must remember you are whole and complete, designed perfectly just the way you are. We are only encouraging a rearranging of priorities and values, not changing the qualities of who you are. Focus your affirmations and prayers on wholeness, on accepting, loving, and cherishing yourself, and *on challenging the very deep beliefs of inadequacy. Rearrange these things. Remember also that humility, openness, and vulnerability are important for your growth, learning, and exchange of consciousness, knowledge, and information with others. Notice carefully that humility and vulnerability are not the same as inadequacy. Shift and release the inadequacy. Embrace self-trust and self-love. Embrace trust and love as part of the perfection and divinity of the universe. You are a part of a bigger puzzle.*

The core message of "choose love and joy" resonated strongly over and over for many months. The concepts of love and joy were so attractive and captivating, so simple and wonderful. I couldn't understand why it was so difficult to get to these states and why I couldn't hold on to them for more than a few minutes. There were so many fearful thoughts, life events, and other people constantly hindering my ability to remain in the states of love and joy. I would later learn that while it was tempting to blame others for my emotional states, it was terribly inaccurate and misleading. I alone was responsible for my internal states.

Of course, the blessing and the curse of being connected with celestial companions was that it provided an indescribable peace and unconditional love unmatched by any other relationship that could ever exist with another human being on the earth. So, I relished my time alone, with only the light beings by my side. At this point in the journey, this introversion helped me capture moments of loving self-acceptance. Many wonderful, long hikes—entire days spent in quality time with my own spirit—were just the medicine I needed to focus my effort towards developing self-compassion.

In addition to developing compassion for my peculiarities, it was time to get curious (instead of angry) about my self-critical and judgmental nature. This gentler approach invited a new understanding—the protective function of my ego was still fiercely active, still trying to keep me safe. For what is criticism and judgment if not a lack of full understanding and an attempt to protect the fragility of what our mind holds true? From here, self-compassion slowly seeded the first sprouts of self-love. Feeling the invisible support of nearby guardians, I began to feel whole in these brief excursions with myself.

Move forward with love. Always move forward with love. Listen to your heart. Be kind, wise, and respectful of others, but also of yourself. Be honest with your feelings and set intentions for your own growth and expansion, yet respect where you are in the moment. Please have compassion and patience with yourself. Be fully aware of your body and your breath. Accept and respect the feelings and sensations that move through you. Be honest, be true, be free. There is no more need for pretending. There is no more need for hiding. It really is okay to be yourself.

Be humble in knowing your relationship with yourself and with others will require work, compromise, forgiveness, and quieting of the ego. You will find the balance. Call on us anytime, and we will support you, remind you, and show you the way—the way of love, the way of wisdom, and the way to align with the frequency of your soul. Love is allowing. Love is receiving. Love is commitment. Love is operating beyond ego. Love is sharing. Love is forgiveness. Love is the most powerful force in the world. It is gentle. It withstands. It is within you. Find it within others. Connect with it. Honor it. Look for it. Value it. Understand it to be important. Do not be afraid of it. There is no need to hide from it. Tap into it within yourself, then look for it and be drawn to it in others.

While I was learning to love and honor myself and strengthening my intuitive connection with an omniscient source, Michael was affixing to more and more rigid external rules and regulations to connect with God through the Jewish Orthodox path. Along with his strict religious views,

Michael was a cellular and molecular metabolic scientist with well over 200 publications and patents. He was also editing an international nutrition journal at the time. I believed his logic-based mind couldn't possibly understand what I was going through, so I mostly avoided the conversation and stayed angry, resentful, and shut-off.

At this point, Michael wore a *kippah* (the Jewish head covering, also known as a *yarmulke*), and he had become *shomer Shabbos*. This meant he strictly observed the Sabbath from sundown on Friday through sundown on Saturday. During the Sabbath period, he didn't use electricity, make or accept phone calls or texts, drive a car, use commerce, or write. He had also adopted the practice of *kashrut*, which was a stringent adherence to only allowing kosher foods in the home that contained the rabbinical *hechsher* designation. As the survivor of two organized religions, a fervent foodie, and the leader of treatment centers espousing psychological flexibility over rigidity, this universal setup blew my mind. There was a pronounced and exaggerated discrepancy in our paths, as is often the case with individual spiritual life lessons. As a wife and mother, I felt abandoned and dismissed—my essence at odds with what my husband was passionately embracing.

What may seem to be random, in the moment, never ever is. It is our job, duty, pleasure, and joy to set the world stage around you to answer your questions, to support you, and to provide inspiration and guidance at every level. Just as the dialogue, connection, and intimacy between partners are so vital to the health of their relationship, opening this dialogue between self and spirit, self and God, and through angels and the counsel of the guides, is vital in the same way. This receiving allows admission of not knowing. It lubricates and speeds learning, growing, and being supported quickly, easily, and in a way that is always available. You are never alone. Never. Whenever you feel confused or concerned, the answer is always easily available to you.

I was harboring anger and resentment because of the fragmented changes in the home, because of how it affected my flow and comfort level, and how it seemed to oppose the clear guidance I had been receiving. Letting go, listening, and plugging into divine communications through the portal of my heart, dissolving the layers of false security and protection to exist exactly as I was—these were my lessons. Nothing else was necessary to experience total peace, oneness, and wisdom. Yet Michael was reaching for outer rituals to know God.

Judgment, criticism, anger, and disconnection clouded interactions with my husband. This path couldn't be right. There was too much duality. I was resentful, brooding, and feeling incredibly stuck. It felt impossible to find common ground. It was much more enticing to spend time in the magnificent, ecstatic dimension. Yet repeatedly, the guides instructed me to bring compassion, love, and forgiveness into the relationship, both for myself and for Michael. Despite this guidance, it took a few long years to process through the anger and hurt and to communicate my honest thoughts and feelings with Michael without yelling or shutting down.

The more you love yourself, the more you respect yourself, and the more you give yourself what you need, the more easily you can do that for another. When you judge yourself, doubt yourself, and dismiss yourself and your needs, then you dismiss the needs of another and expect another to conform. To respect and love what you are, as you are, gives you the compassion, love, and forgiveness to respect what someone else is and needs. To love yourself means to be honest about your own needs and your own evolution. And to love another means to be honest about their needs and their evolution. Interact in love, respect, kindness, compassion, and forgiveness, both with Michael and yourself. Check in with how you feel. That will give you the answer. That will help you map the direction you are going and whether you are moving towards misery or joy.

To connect with the flow of universal energy is to be open, conscious, and clear. To be closed is to be hardened and stuck within the mind, the body, and the self—separated from the Source, from consciousness, the exchange of information, and from the flow. To open is to let go. Let go of control, isolation, shut-down, and thinking that an individual is complete, in and of itself alone.

You already unknowingly practice this energetic exchange every time you connect with another person—opening up, sharing back and forth, allowing one to express an outflow of energy, and then absorb and receive the inflow of energy from the other. When you engage in this process, it is not just the two of you. When you open yourself to create a connection, you are connecting beyond the self and beyond the other person. When you connect, you tap into the stream of energy and consciousness where the Source resides. It is present between two people. It is present with three, four, five people, and more—within any group that is open, sharing, and receiving. This practice of opening up an exchange of energy flow in and out will help inspire you. This is true both in relationship with God, in relationship with one another, and, of course, in relationship with the universal flow that exists all around you.

Once you realize this truth, then whenever you freely express and easily receive, you are opening yourself to God's support, inspiration, and guidance. Even in nonspiritual matters, when you are connecting with another at work, at the store, or any type of interaction, you can understand that we, as your guides, as a conduit from the Creator, speak to you through other people. This happens all the time. When you open yourself to receive from God and from us, we can deliver information to you through any open interchange.

I opened up. We talked. We tried to find a connection, but it felt impossible. One morning, I heard a very clear voice in my meditation. *"Pray for him."* This annoyed me. I was too angry to share my divine connection with the man who brought me so much pain. Hello again, ego.

Holding onto resentment only served to keep me closed off from intimacy and away from the flow of joy and love. I had to let go and forgive, at least for myself, if nothing else. So, I prayed daily for my husband, for my ability to forgive, and for my marriage. And it was through this process I remembered that relationships are two-sided. It wasn't just that Michael had abandoned me in pursuit of his religious ideals; I had also abandoned him in pursuit of my own truth. We both had a lot of emotional unpacking to do.

It took us a while to wade through our complicated feelings and beliefs. But we did. Once Michael and I opened up honestly and tenderly to one another from a place of respect and forgiveness, we began to process through the complicated layers. Each time one of us got activated (which happened often), we had to make the conscious choice to return to respect and return to love. These were, after all, the only core values that would allow us to move forward, he as an Orthodox Jew, and me as, well, me.

Use the energy you have been angrily and anxiously expending for pretending, and turn that into love. Love your soul. Honor who and what you are. Also, honor the soul in others. You must recognize and have compassion every day because so, so, so many others are still asleep and hiding. You must have love and compassion, being careful of judgment, criticism, frustration, and anger. Remember what it was like when your soul was asleep. Remember the pain, suffering, discomfort, and confusion you felt. Your soul was in there, underneath all of that, and the pure Source is living inside other people. Your job, my dear, is to treat others with love and to honor your own soul with love. We ask you to pray, meditate, and sing your heart's song. Accept the frequency of your soul.

Ultimately, I realized I was angrier at myself than at Michael. I had been the one hiding and not expressing my genuine nature. Though his truth was an entire universe away from mine, I was jealous of Michael for unapologetically living out his own unique path. My wild and wonderful heart longed to be free for so many years. I was the one responsible for accepting, loving, and taking care of myself. Michael's own life choices were up to him, and mine were up to me. This was a huge revelation to me, as I had a dangerous pattern of blaming others for my unhappiness and giving away the power that ultimately lies within.

Once I finally accepted and loved all of myself, I felt more grounded, more whole. I found compassion for myself, which helped me find compassion for others. I also finally learned the immeasurable value of honest self-care, which made it easier to honor and respect Michael's unique path. It now felt natural to accept Michael's differences and his need to choose the path that was right for him, just as I accepted my own differences and my need to choose the path that was right for me.

In the end, I had to admit that paradoxically, despite all the new rigid rules in the home, Michael was actually softening. I had just been too angry to notice. He had been embracing the mystical teachings of Orthodox Judaism and was more spiritually connected than ever before. It finally struck me: Michael had never wavered from unconditionally loving me, despite our vast, overwhelming differences. He had been right there all along.

Once I relaxed my protective layer of indignation, I again saw Michael as the maverick I once fell in love with. I saw the other side of his personality, the one that was responsible for his many scientific discoveries. It was this progressive and innovative trait that allowed for our non-traditional marriage. This shift in perspective—this reminder that we had once vowed respect, acceptance, and love as our core values—led us both directly back to a shared platform. After all the years of separate and intensely divergent paths, we were returning back to love, back to togetherness. This miraculous reunion was completely mind-blowing and truly humbling.

REMAINING HUMBLE

There is a great depth of experience within the silence. There are multiple layers in the physical, emotional, and spiritual realms. In fact, there is more happening in any moment than you could ever take in and absorb. You will only take in that which you are open to receiving. Right now, you are only perceiving a tiny window of all that exists around and within you.

You have learned you can shift your vibration. You can open yourself to different energetic frequencies, and with practice, you will be able to do this at will. But now, without even trying, simply observe and recognize the enormous depth of the human experience. Observe in quiet, in curiosity, in any moment. Play with this. Recognize what you are perceiving and experiencing. Then, as soon as you identify your mental, physical, and emotional state, raise or lower, deepen or lessen, constrict or expand your energy to experience something at a different vibrational frequency. Play with this practice and have fun doing it. Let yourself move in and out and up and down the continuum of energetic states.

Remember, there is no better or worse. When you judge, you miss opportunities, influences, observations, and lessons. As soon as you do this, you limit your spectrum of perception. You must understand that experiencing expanded consciousness allows you to move through frequencies and environments. There is no greater or lesser. Understand that different moments require distinct energies. Remember that you are one with all. You are not separate. You are not greater. You must remain humble. Be comfortable and fluid at every energetic frequency, not just at that which you perceive to be the highest.

This energy flow is happening all the time, whether you are aware of it or not. You think you can feel the energy when you are meditating or praying, and that is wonderful. But realize the life force is moving through you when you don't even know it—when your ego doesn't know it. Living your life totally obliviously, the stream of universal energy moves through you (and others) in ways you do not yet understand. You cannot get wrapped into any ego because it is not you.

Release any arrogance around this, and instead, practice humility. Embrace humility and embrace the mystery. Remember, there is more to all of this than your intellectual mind can comprehend in this life. Just let it go. Don't worry about it. Don't stress. It is not about you, and you cannot fully understand it. With this path, my darling, you will feel such a deep sense of harmony and fulfillment. You will feel deep contentment and satisfaction in your life, your purpose, and your work. This is a path of humility and mystery. The entire universe is at your fingertips, moving through you, and your only job is to allow—to step out of the way.

You understand the incredible power of slowing down to recognize the subtle lessons for yourself and others. Slow down, release control, and trust that which is beyond you. Don't be so eager to grab on to Source energy and wield it for your own personal gain. Instead, allow the energy to guide you. Don't open up just long enough to receive it, and then immediately attempt to control it. Don't try to repackage it. Rather, become a servant of it.

There was increasingly less discrepancy between my altered and ordinary states of consciousness. Meaningful visions became commonplace in my meditations and my dreams, similar to the revelations during tongue-speak. Synchronicities were popping up with remarkable frequency. Symbols and images were dancing through my life, inviting me onto the psyche's creative path to consciousness. Sometimes, they appeared as precognitions, sometimes as insights that emerged instantaneously; other times, they took days, weeks, or months to interpret and comprehend. I wanted to learn more. I wanted to explore the purpose and meaning behind these epiphanies and invitations.

I began studying with a talented Jungian analyst who helped me break down, decipher, and honor the wisdom and teachings embedded within the striking symbolism and set stages of life's everyday moments. This spiritual-intellectual work allowed me to connect with the same wisdom I experienced through the altered states of consciousness in everyday waking life. Meaning and inspiration were everywhere and in everyone—perceivable in this physical earthly dimension of reality.

The everyday flow of divine consciousness was unquestionably less intense and ecstatic than the tongue-speaking classroom sessions, but it was still the same flow of wisdom and guidance, nonetheless. I learned to feel, sense, remain curious, and connect—while in an everyday, awakened, embodied state—to the seen, the unseen, my own spirit, and the Source outside of myself. I learned to listen deeply as one fully-integrated being, living in physical, intellectual, and spiritual worlds simultaneously. Though the power was less magnified, and the connection far more subtle, I learned to see with eyes wide open, just as I had learned to see in a trance state with my eyes closed.

I learned the stream of divine energy and information is multi-faceted and deeply intertwined, instructing and responding as a creative flow of consciousness from both within and without. This flow was accessible in the spiritual classroom, but also in conference rooms and meetings, living rooms and bedrooms, spreadsheets and prayers, on hikes, family dinners, and in happenstance conversations with strangers. The ordinary moments became sacred. I marveled in taking it all in—not just the tongue-speak, the shamanic ecstasy, my dreams and emotions, the energy moving through my body, or the symbols from my visions. All of it created the amazingly sophisticated, yet astoundingly simple, fabric of spirit—an enlivened, ubiquitous force from both within and without.

I was beginning to feel like one integrated being. A subtle, yet palpable, dissolution occurred in my perceived duality. Aha! My ego and soul had always been separate parts of one whole; I just hadn't been able to realize it until now.

Allow the flow of consciousness to enter and move through you completely. Let it guide you. Allow guidance from the spirit and guidance from your soul. Surrender completely. You will find so much more happiness and peace than you could ever imagine by allowing the Source to guide you, move through you, and carry you forward in your life. The practice is simple. You must surrender to the Source, yet you must also remember that you are one with the Source. Do not confuse this. Do not think that you must use divine energy to be a co-creator. Instead, allow divine energy to use you. Allow yourself to be one with all. Open and receive equally. When you vibrate at the frequency of divine consciousness, the world opens for you, and you can connect with it everywhere you go.

If I am to surrender completely, then my ultimate truth, my totality, likely will evolve over time. Consciousness seems to be alive and formless, responding and interacting, moving forward towards wholeness. So perhaps all I can do is remain humbly attuned and follow the guidance as it comes, rather than attaching my identity to labels and certainties.

BATHING IN THE LIGHT

When I did cross over to the other dimension through tongue-speak, I always felt suspended in a yellowish-white light substance that seemed to change my physical body. Though difficult to describe, it felt like bathing in a pure light treatment, a sort of ethereal medicine to the cells of my being.

We have only scratched the surface of understanding energy, consciousness, and the realm that lies beyond this physical world. You are learning to lift the veil and enter the dimension of infinity. You are also learning that the body is an energy system, and you can feel the intensity of flow emanating through your palms when you slow down, plug in, pray, or meditate. This intense current of white light is very different than anything you have experienced before. The quality of this energy is indescribably powerful, yet gentle in its strength and stability. This healing white light is smooth and subtle. It is the invisible substance that flows in prayer and in healing. This substance is real, and you can learn to feel it, sense it, and guide it for the healing of yourself and others.

When you pray, you can direct this energy. Project this white light from your mind's eye or from your heart center. Imagine the person, situation, or event for which you are praying. Surround this person, event, or situation in a brilliant healing light. When you pray in this way, you do not need to add cognitive intention. When you struggle with prayer, how to pray for a person, or what to pray for beyond general healing and your own safety, simply see the person, event, or situation in your imagination, and allow the Source to flow towards the object of your prayer. That is all.

Remember to get out of your own way. Give the mental chatter of your mind a break and just sit with the light. Realize that this stream of healing energy contains its own consciousness and knows exactly what to do. It is not your doing. You, as a person, are not doing anything. You are only allowing. You are holding the space and directing the stream where to flow. Then you step back and let it do its work. Allow, feel the energy, and notice what it's doing. You will feel and sense when it has *passed, and you can move to the next person, event, or situation for which you want to pray.*

You will recognize it has a rhythm of its own, and in this way, you are following it. You are a partner with this energy, this divine flow, this Source which you do not understand. It is very important for you to understand you are not creating this Source energy. You are working in partnership to guide the flowing light. In this work, humility is of paramount importance. Humility is the very most important element when allowing your physical body to be a spiritual portal.

Your greatest gift allows. Become familiar with the sensations of this energy flowing through you and allow this to be your guiding light. Do not be afraid to heal yourself. Just as you pray for the healing of others, do not be shy to use this energy on your own self, your own psyche, and your own body. This is a simple reminder, an invitation that prayer is an important practice for you—your ability to connect to this Source is something to use every day without fear.

I had been meditating for twenty years at this point, and I had practiced prayer from a very young age. But this was different. It was a blend of meditative prayer, both concentrating and surrendering, using both a focused mind and an open heart in concert with one another. It felt like a symbiotic partnership as opposed to me concentrating or praying to achieve a specific outcome. This had less pressure, less doing, and more allowing. It was peaceful and trusting. It felt like home.

In a guided session with my mother, after we visited with some family who had passed, she asked if we could connect with Jesus. I had not communicated with this master since my adolescent years when I was a practicing Christian. But just like clockwork, the connection was effortless, and the answers to our questions came flowing through. Since that time, several others have asked to connect with spiritual or religious figures. These masters are always happy to show up and share their wisdom and love—an indescribably beautiful experience. They have taught of healing, working with the light, the power of prayer, and what things are like in the heavenly realm. They truly seem delighted to offer guidance and direction to those who ask.

When you meditate and recognize energy moving from your palms, that stream, that flow is living. Healing energy is not inert. It is alive. It carries consciousness. It carries information. It carries intelligence. Jesus is a master of this energy.

Prayer comes from the mind and the heart. It is an output of energy. Just as thoughts contribute to creating reality, so prayer contributes to spiritual assistance. When crying out for the help of angels, guides, and spiritual masters, know that they receive the call. It is like calling them on the phone or sending an email. To pray is to send energy, and those prayers always have an answer. However, people often do not recognize or accept the answer when they are not tuned in to receive or when they cannot acknowledge the answer they do not want to hear.

Prayer works beyond time and space. This work is precious to the great spiritual masters. Realize there is no conflict when so many people pray because there is no time where they are. They hear and receive prayers from all who call out to them for help and guidance. These spirits work within individual lives. They touch people's hearts and minds.

Jesus, saints, and other spiritual masters can direct healing to people who are currently living. Likewise, living people can send healing energy across dimensions. You can send healing energy to anyone in the spiritual realm, and it is received and appreciated. This type of healing prayer has the same value as when a spiritual master sends it to you. The perceived value of a soul does not generate the value of the healing energy. One who has mastered vibration and knows how to work with energy is more efficient, and the vibration is more directed and concentrated. But as for the intention of the healing energy, it doesn't matter who it is coming from.

We are all energy. We all have the energy to heal and positively impact each other, and this is an important practice. Integrating prayer for others into your life is perhaps one of the most important things you do all day. The impact is very, very real. It is just as important as sending an email or having a business meeting. Prayer for yourself and for others in your life—family, friends, business colleagues, clients, and even people you barely have a relationship with—deepens your connection with Source and changes the vibration in which you move through the world. This shift in vibration affects the energetic exchange you have with other people, with the world around you, and with yourself.

Prayer is not glamorous. Yet prayer strengthens your connection with us, your own spiritual self, your intuition, and with infinite intelligence—with divine consciousness, that sense of calm, clear knowing. Meditation is very, very important. Meditation affects and shifts your energy, your psyche, and what happens in your inner landscape. Do not stop meditating. Continue full force with consistency. Meditation is key, yet intentional prayer is even more important for you and for your path. Prayer is a way to contribute and give back. Prayer is your homework. Remember, there is no time and space in prayer. You can pray in the present, the past, or in the future. It is one of the most magical, impactful things you can do. We are here to guide you in this effort. We are available to you as your prayer partners. Enjoy this process with us.

STORIES AND PERSPECTIVES

Over the course of this strange journey, I slowly shared parts of it with those closest to me. As companions and witnesses, four very different people offer their own perspectives in the following pages. The first story was contributed by my best friend and shamanic partner, Dr. Annie Wills, a clinical psychologist of twenty-five years who repeatedly connected with her deceased parents during our work together. The second perspective was written by my husband, Dr. Michael Zemel, an orthodox Jew and a cellular and molecular scientist. The third perspective was written by the woman who birthed and raised me, a devout

Christian, Paula Jacobs. The fourth story was contributed by my big sister, Kerry Page, a trauma survivor who shared a connection with our grandmother.

ANNIE: CONNECTING WITH MY PARENTS

The most beautiful, heartbreaking experience of my life was being with my father when he died. My mother and sister shared this moment with me. We all sat around his hospital bed set up in my parents' living room, holding hands. About a month after he passed, my mother, sister, and I were at my parents' home when the phone rang. Before picking it up, I peeked at the caller ID out of old habit. My dad's name was displayed on the screen. My heart sank. Wait, how could this be? The display listed his name and the home phone number—the number for the same line that was ringing. I froze, looked at my mom and sister then said, "It's Dad." Chills moved down my spine as I picked up the phone. No one was there.

Shortly after that, I asked Siri if she thought we could connect with him using her gift. Not only were we able to talk with him that day, but we made the connection several more times in the years to follow, as well as after my mother passed away. These connections were reassuring. It

— STORIES AND PERSPECTIVES —

was as if my parents really were right there with us. When Siri channeled their presence, her demeanor completely shifted, and sometimes tears rolled down her cheeks. I could tell she was overwhelmed with emotion, and she was truly sensing my parents. As a clinical psychologist for the past twenty-five years, I had no doubt we were making an emotional connection in these encounters. It was hard not being able to see or touch them, but the communications were still comforting. Not a single time did our attempt to connect fail. Every time we reached out, something happened.

Sometimes Siri cried, sometimes she laughed, and other times she was gentle or stern, depending on the message being relayed. In addition to regularly communicating with both of my parents, we reached out to a few of my dear friends who had passed away. Whenever we connected with my friend, Dana, Siri's energy was excited, buoyant, and somehow mobile, just like Dana. But when we connected with my dad, Siri's energy became still, comfortable, and quiet, just like his.

Of all the lessons and conversations, one stands out in my memory above the rest. I personally struggle with seasonal affective disorder, and in the winter months, grief and sadness overcome me. I want to connect with my parents when Siri isn't around. My dad and mom left their physical bodies five and two years ago, respectively. Even though they have told me they are with me, sometimes the grief becomes an unbearable fog that is impossible to see through. Siri and I always began each session with a prayer to protect and guide the work:

> We call on our guides to fill the space with light and love and healing, with clarity and connection, with clear communication, and with divine intervention and guidance to answer our questions and give us support and information to move forward in our healing. We set the intention and clear the space only for light and love and healing. Clear out any doubt, fear, negativity, anxiety, and ego that may interfere or block the process of communication—both giving and receiving. Clear our hearts and minds for pure communication to remove as many of our own filters and fears as possible.

After a moment or two of silence, the message began.

Know that loss is only at the human level. There is no loss at the soul level. Your soul is still connected just as much as before. It always will be. It is ok that you are experiencing grief. It is part of the sacred human experience. Yet grief can also be like a gremlin. It can have a darkness to it that seductively pulls you in, but grief, in itself, is ok. It is natural. But since grief can also pull you in, you must be careful of it.

They (your parents) do not experience grief. That is not where they vibrate. If you can, move through the grief because when it grabs hold of you, it can be difficult to get out. Allow it, but then move through it if you can. They (parents) say, "call us" if you get stuck in the grief and you need a lifeline. They cannot be with you in the grief, but they can help you out of it if you ask. But if you stay in the grief, they cannot meet you there.

There is a vision of a deep, dark hole or cave. They (parents) are at the top in the light, and you are at the bottom, in the dark, stuck with the gremlin of grief. They cannot come down, but they can throw you a rope from the top. They can let down a rope or a ladder, or even an escalator if you want it to be easier. You can choose how you would like to get out. You can ask them for help in this way. But before you grab the rope or take the first step to come out, you must disengage with the gremlin that is holding you in grief. You must disengage with it, and then you can move towards the light and reconnect, and they said they love it when they can reconnect with you.

They (parents) say, "Please, my dear, be gentle and understand we can only communicate with you in very soft and subtle ways.

We are not communicators that can cross to the human mind, and your design is also not as a communicator to cross dimensions. So, for this to work, like what we are doing now in this conversation, we need to have a channel designed for this work."

But they (parents) can speak to you in very subtle ways—in ways that you may wonder are real. Please understand the delicacy, gentleness, and subtleness of what that communication will feel like. It could be a thought. It could be a very, very brief image or memory. It could be that someone you don't even know says something that reminds you of them or uses a phrase they used to say. Or maybe you have a dream. Or maybe you have a feeling. They say the following:

> It is time to uncouple the grief when these things happen. Recognize we are trying to communicate with you, but when these things happen, you get roped by the gremlin, and you get sad. We did not want you to feel sad and separated. Our intent was always to be with you. Take delight in our presence. As small as it may feel, when you have a memory of us, smile at the memory because we have given that to you. We are connected with you in that memory. We are connected in that thought, but as soon as you get roped back into sadness and grief, we lose our connection with you. We lose the touch of you. Not physical touch, but touch in light. It is a touchpoint in the light.

Siri later described to me the visions she experienced during the session. First, the vision of me in a dark cave with a gremlin, and my parents up in the light, offering different forms of assistance to help me come towards the light. Next, Siri saw an image of their hands reaching for me in a fully whitelit backdrop. As I moved into the light, they could connect with me, but as I moved out of the light, they lost the ability to touch me.

Ask yourself this very simply, 'Is the feeling light, or is the feeling dark?' If the thought of us, our memory, a reminder, or a feeling is light, even if for only a few seconds, we ask you to appreciate and enjoy those few seconds. Remain in the whiteness as long as you comfortably can. When it turns dark and black and sad, know that we aren't there anymore. It's a process for you in your own spiritual development to struggle back towards the light. And we will continue to invite as many light experiences as we can. But please be gentle; these experiences will be subtle, but know we are there.

In my personal experience over the past several years and after dozens of "classroom" sessions with Siri, I am left feeling hopeful, peaceful, and sure about the presence of divine love. I realize I don't have to be afraid of death, and I will reunite with my loved ones again. I realize I am still connected with them, even now. This entire journey has clarified and solidified for me that we are all one, and we are all love. I have learned it all comes down to the heart. That's where the connection is, where the soul lives, and who we really are. We are unconditional love.

MICHAEL: PERSPECTIVES AS A SCIENTIST, JEW, AND WITNESS

You already know a bit about me from the preceding chapters—that I can be characterized as a highly-rational scientist (for better or for worse), and I'm also an observant Jew. I concede that both of these roles involve a lot of rules, so I suppose my life doesn't sound very spiritual, but in truth, it is all supported by intensely mystical underpinnings. I can offer my perspective from both vantage points, but also from a third, as a witness. You see, I have watched Siri's journey unfold and evolve over the past fifteen years of our marriage.

The first time I heard Siri speak her language, it was very early in our marriage, and I had no idea what (if anything) to make of it. It just came spilling out of her in a half-awake state as she looked at me and spoke earnestly, clearly communicating. I don't know what she was saying, but it was certainly something! Over time, with repeated occurrences, usually in the middle of the night or when Siri became startled, I came to understand the smallest fraction of simple statements, and it was truly remarkable! This was obviously not gibberish, even though I couldn't understand it. This was a clear form of language, which seemed to resonate with its own grammar and structural patterns. At this point, I couldn't understand, and Siri couldn't translate yet. Over time, Siri and I came to wonder if this was in some way linked to her growing interest in past life regression. Could this be a language leftover from a past life? It was as good an explanation as any other. In the meantime, the frequency and duration of these language episodes increased.

"What language does your wife speak?" A recovery room nurse asked me as Siri came out of anesthesia after a minor surgical procedure. I didn't know the answer—how could I? Siri didn't know either. But she did come to know, understand, and interpret, offering me glimpses as she became comfortable doing so over time.

What do I think of all of this? The short answer is that I simply don't know. The better answer is that it's complicated. We all see things through our own filters. Am I fully rational, believing only in what I can see, touch, and verify? Or am I spiritual, accepting truths I cannot touch?

Who made up the rules, this dichotomy? Why can't I be both? I am both. I am a scientist, but I'm also a spiritual person. As a scientist, I believe in generating and testing ideas, running experiments, assessing the data, and generating new ideas in an ongoing spiral, moving towards *an* objective truth (not *the* objective truth). There's more. There is always more.

In my case, my spiritual side is expressed through orthodox Judaism. The notion that science and spirituality must be at odds is a myth. They can and should be in partnership, and while you will certainly find scientists who are atheists, you will also find many scientists deeply connected to their faith as Jews, Christians, Moslems, Sikhs, and others. Paraphrasing the late Rabbi Jonathan Sacks, science can tell you *what* happens, religion can tell you *why*. All of this to say that no, my being a rational scientist does not cause me to question Siri's gift. In fact, it saddens me she felt the need to keep it hidden for so many years.

Does this mean I believe in the existence of spirit guides and that one can be gifted with the ability to communicate with them? I think what's more important is that I do believe it *could* be real and true; indeed, I have no better explanation. How does this square with my Jewish beliefs? I see no conflict. As a Jew, I believe souls have an existence both before entering and after leaving the body. Kabbalah (Jewish mysticism) teaches us many are reincarnated to complete unfinished tasks, so why wouldn't it be possible for there to be communication between life and the afterlife? There are certainly Jewish biblical examples of such communication, although not favorably described.

Have I taken advantage of Siri's gift (or would I do so) to contact loved ones who are no longer here? The answer has been "no." Why? In part because I don't need it. Those whose souls are no longer connected to their bodies are where they need to be, and that remains so, whether I communicate with them or not. Wherever they are, in a dimension beyond time and space, I can't shake the notion that if they wanted to openly communicate with me—indeed, if they were *meant* to communicate with me, then they would. Perhaps they will yet, I don't know, but I don't feel comfortable pushing it from my side of the divide. That's a personal decision, and I don't know if my perspective on this is of much consequence.

What matters is that I fully support my wife and her evolution towards wholeness, whatever that means for her. I support her quest to understand and master this gift, as well as her responsible use of it in ways that bring joy, relief, and peace to herself and others, just as it has done for our family.

PAULA: THROUGH THE EYES OF A CHRISTIAN MOTHER

I raised Siri with a Christian worldview that acknowledged miracles. She often heard the story of my inexplicable survival at age nineteen. I had a rare yet lethal complication from mononucleosis: the spontaneous rupture of my spleen. Through a series of medical errors, three days of transfused blood filled my belly, and a mere pint of blood flowed through my veins. It was a clinical picture inconsistent with life. Yet what science seeks to explain through logic, faith accepts as divine mercy and grace. What I did not tell the surgeon, nor even my parents, was that God visited me in my intensive care bed, explaining that my trip to heaven would have to wait. That brief, peaceful, light-filled, and comforting encounter with the Father shaped my faith and laid the foundation for what I would teach my children. Synthesizing that experience has taken a lifetime.

I couldn't fully comprehend the depth of God's affection until I first held my own child in my arms, literally bursting with pure, unconditional love. Jesus prayed for his followers to enjoy the same perfect unity that he enjoyed with the Father, "as you, Father, are in me and I am in you, may they also be in us." (John 17:23). During those brief, miraculous moments in the hospital room all those years ago, I could see myself through God's eyes and love myself through God's heart. Paradise is real, with comfort and acceptance beyond mortal understanding. My desire to be with our Father in heaven was stronger than anything I'd ever felt. Yet through shared understanding—that perfect unity—we agreed that it wasn't my time.

Siri learned to love a living God who loves us more than we can imagine—a God who is merciful and just, and who wants us to know Him. Jesus promised we would not be left as orphans and that the Advocate, the Holy Spirit, would be sent in His name to teach us everything we need to know and to remind us of His words (John 14:18).

In her preschool years, Siri stated her dream of being a saint when she grew up. When I pointed out that saints often endure much suffering, she was unfazed. She showed a deep love for God, receiving special permission to be one of the youngest lectors in our Catholic church at age fourteen. But immediately after high school graduation, a mission trip to Zimbabwe introduced her to a brand of fundamentalist Christianity that countered her belief in God's unconditional love for the vast, disparate community of His children, and she sought another path.

Siri became drawn to the transcendental—yoga, meditation, and the Sikh religion. This seemed to be a natural progression of Siri's spirituality. Thus, at age twenty-three, my Jill Kristen (translated as "Christian girl") became Siri-Datar (translated as "great infinite giver"). It was admittedly quite painful to see my daughter move away from a faith her father and I spent years nurturing. But faith is the most personal experience anyone can have, and I knew this had to be her journey, not ours.

When meditative chants heightened her strange, indecipherable language, Siri was uncertain what to make of it. Speaking in tongues was not a routine part of the worship experience in our Catholic church. I had never told Siri that years prior, a dear church friend invited me to attend a "baptism of the spirit" at an evangelical-leaning Episcopal church. Surrounded by several prayerful women laying hands on me, my spirit released similar utterances, interpreted by others there as, "Only in God do I find safety." That experience stuck with me for years. While I was never quite sure if it was the spirit talking or just my imagination, the thought of finding safety in God served as a comfort.

The apostle Paul was the foremost expert on the topic, writing, "For those who speak in a tongue do not speak to other people but to God; for nobody understands them, since they are speaking mysteries in the Spirit" (1 Cor 14:1). Paul referred to his worship through tongues as praying with his spirit and connecting with the spirit in a way that surpasses verbal understanding. When viewed from that context, it seems both reasonable and reassuring that prayer punctuated by speaking in tongues always precedes Siri's connection to the spiritual realm.

Special revelation—those miraculous means God uses to reveal Himself—was an accepted concept in our home. The Bible is full of examples of God appearing in physical form, sending messenger angels, and speaking through dreams. Yet many today seem to consider those to be ancient, even superstitious, approaches and scoff at any notion of God presenting Himself so overtly in modern theology. On the contrary, most of my life decisions have been guided by special revelation: finding my husband, guiding my career, facing fear, accepting hardships as gifts, and nurturing my faith. What many consider fanciful mysticism remains an inherent part of my Christian belief system.

It always surprises me to come across church leaders who doubt the level of intimacy God wants with his faithful and, instead, attribute a loving, spiritual presence to an evil force. It is ironic because rejection of the active presence of the Holy Spirit by those who wish to be righteous is what Matthew labeled as the "unforgivable sin" (Matthew 12:31-32).

That being said, when Siri first offered a session to connect with my departed loved ones via a spiritual connection, I was skeptical. As one who has always relied deeply on daily prayer and guidance from the Holy Spirit to make it through life, intimate communion with the Father was second nature. But inviting exposure to an unknown spirit was unsettling. Echoes from Isaiah regarding the foolhardiness of consulting ghosts for teaching and instruction gave me significant pause. But did not God's messenger angels guide Lot from Sodom? Did not Gabriel announce himself as one who stood in the presence of God, sent to share some pretty exciting news with Zacharias? And did this same angel not instruct Joseph to be an earthly protector of our beloved Mary and Jesus? Because I had watched Siri's sincere and prayerful journey into the mystical over many years, I agreed to give it a try, prayerfully asking for divine protection throughout the process.

To my great relief, each experience has been profound. In every case, the experience was full of love, wonder, and joy. In each of these experiences, it has been no surprise that the most present participant has been my father because it has been commonplace for me to feel his presence since he passed away in 1981. He has appeared in my dreams and through many signs—those uncanny, unlikely coincidences that assured me he was still watching over me, comforting me with his supernatural presence. When we spoke in the spirit through Siri, he assured me that, yes, he was always nearby. What an amazing gift this has been! And my Aunt Martha, the most recent to enter heaven in 2016, was so excited to tell me about heavenly wonders she could barely contain herself. Never a particularly strong practitioner of faith, she kept repeating, "You won't believe it. You just won't believe it! It's so wonderful here!"

Each loved one I have spoken to in the spirit has painted the same picture of life in the eternal. There is no sense of time, but there is still work to be done. Personal and spiritual growth is still in progress. There are angels who stand ready to be with us when we cry out for help. We are not alone. But most importantly, we are loved.

My prayer for Siri is for her to continue using this gift to help others come to the understanding that God is always with us. We are His children, going through this life experience together. We are each accountable to do His will to the best of our abilities and to love each other. We each are obligated to follow the great commission on earth, "thy will be done, on earth as it is in heaven," to help all recognize and accept the glory of God, our Father. These are not just words in a prayer; this is our charge.

Over the years, I have said there are just a few things of which I am certain. I am certain there is a God and that He loves us. I am certain that Jesus came to teach us about our Father and to show us how to be one with Him. I am certain that the Holy Spirit was sent to be our comforter, to be with us always. And beyond that, I am certain there is a lot I do not know. For now, my faith rests on the unshakable knowledge that we are children of a living God, and we are loved beyond human understanding.

KERRY: TELLING MY SECRET TO OUR GRANDMOTHER

I mentioned to my sister (Siri) how much I missed our grandmother, Nonny, and how I wished I could connect with her in some way. I carried this wish for the past thirty-eight years, ever since the night my mother told me she died of cancer. I was in the second grade. I loved my grandmother immensely, and her passing left a hole in my heart. I spent the last thirty-eight years talking to her daily, wishing she could hear me, but I never got any sort of response.

I wanted to feel her warm hug and soft embrace again. I wanted to hear her laugh and taste her wonderful food. I wanted her to know I loved to cook, just like she did, and I wanted her to be proud of the woman I had become. But most of all, I wanted Nonny to know my secret—the secret I tried so hard to tell her when I was a small child and never could. The secret I cried about every night during my formative years. The secret that had been festering inside of me since the day it became a big secret.

I almost got the courage to tell her one night while my parents were away, when I was around six years old. I practiced the words repeatedly in my head to say it *just right* because I was scared I would be in trouble for what happened. "That man down the street touched me. He touched my private parts. He made me do bad things." Those words just kept spinning in my head, repeatedly, like a broken record, every night, for weeks and months. The words were there, but I couldn't say them out loud.

Nonny died about a year later, and I was never able to tell her my secret. I was also never able to come to terms with what had happened to me or to understand I wasn't an awful, terrible, horrible girl for letting him do those things to me. I spent years struggling with intense pain fused with self-hatred, anxiety, depression, and eating disorders.

— GUIDED —

One evening while we were dining at a nearby Italian restaurant, I mentioned to my sister that I would love to talk to Nonny. Her immediate response was, "Well, we can make the call and see what happens, but I can't promise anything." When she said that, fear ran through me. Make the call? Call Nonny? I knew that Siri had a special gift because she had done a few sessions with our mother over the last few years, and I suppose, on some level, that's why I casually floated the topic. But I wasn't sure how I actually felt about the idea. Would we be opening some unknown portal for spirits to get out? What would happen, exactly? Would this be a big mistake I would regret later? There were a million questions running through my head, and frankly, I was terrified.

Siri and I had been siblings for the past forty-three years. We'd been together for a very long time, through good times and bad. I knew her well, very possibly better than almost anyone else on the planet. However, I knew nothing about her gift and had never experienced it in all of our years together. I did remember her having fun and playing with her imaginary friends as a kid, and I was always jealous because I didn't have any imaginary friends myself. I remember tea parties in our little shared bedroom, complete with a table, chairs, and stuffed animals all around. We set up our little teacups and saucers around the table, and Siri spoke to all of her imaginary friends in another strange language. She had fully developed her gift and started using it only in the past few years.

The words "we can make the call" kept repeating in my head. My anxiety activated and was getting worse by the minute. I felt my chest tightening, and I was unsure if I should go through with it or not. By the time we returned to my parents' house, where Siri was staying, the fear took over. We went to a bedroom in the back of the house and closed the door to drown out the noise of children and pets running around. Siri sat cross-legged on the bed, and I sat beside her. My insides were shaking.

As Siri began, she explained the process to me gently. She said her eyes would be closed, and she would open up with a prayer. She explained this would be a very sacred experience, it wasn't within her control, and we would simply put ourselves in a state of receptivity. She asked if I wanted to proceed, and I heard myself say, "Yes."

Siri clarified that her guides often gave her messages right away. Those would be for her, and the later messages would be for me. She also told me she would try and establish a connection, but her guides had previously explained that souls have the choice to reincarnate or remain in the spiritual realm, so she didn't know if we would be able to communicate with Nonny or not.

As I was sitting on the bed, shaking but trying to keep myself together, Siri sat up straight, tall and confident, her legs crossed. She placed her hands on her lap and became very quiet. She sat in silence, looking very calm, while I could feel my heart beating in my chest. A minute or two went by, and it seemed like time stood still. Then, my sister began to speak quietly, but not in a language I understood. It reminded me of the language she spoke when we were little, during our tea parties with her imaginary friends.

She began very slowly and intentionally, speaking the strange words and interpreting as she went along. As Siri spoke, her entire face lit up, and she was smiling from ear to ear. She radiated peace and love beyond anything I had ever experienced with her before. Her voice was soft yet firm as she began:

The way—it is not about trying harder. It's just about doing it differently. It's about changing the frequency at which you receive and dropping your energy out of your mind of thought, worry, and anxiety. We encourage you to spend more time in prayer and in meditation. Come to this place frequently. Visit us. Sit within this frequency to receive peace, healing, knowledge, and information. Receive it for yourself, your life, and your loved ones to uplift—to create hope and healing in the world. We open this path to you. We only ask that you show up, and we will pave the way. Show up and come here. Learn to sit within the flames, the fire, the energy, the information—to learn, to grow, to experience in this new and different way, to feel and allow. Do not be afraid.

This guidance was not what I had asked for, but I desperately needed to hear it. One constant trait I had displayed in my life was always trying *so hard*. No matter what I accomplished, it was never enough. I had spent my life trying to show people I really *was* a good girl, after all. I wasn't the awful, terrible girl I believed I was because of the things I let that big man do to me when I was little. I was a good girl, and I'd spent my entire life trying to prove it.

It felt as though a parent was speaking directly to me, telling me it was OK. I could stop trying so hard. I could just *be*. These words gave me immense comfort and knowing. Siri continued with the messages she was receiving.

Allow the veil to be lifted and the light to shine through the darkness. The darkness for you is fear and doubt, the depths of worry and shame. The light is there, and it can and will pierce through. It is not about trying. It is not about reaching. It is not about strength or skill. It is the opposite. It is about allowing complete surrender. Letting go. Release the grip of the illusion of control. Release the grip of trying and striving. It's more of an exhale. Let go. Trust.

After receiving these messages, my fear fully subsided. I knew it was no accident that I was in that bedroom with her at that moment, receiving the exact messages I needed. I was relieved. I was relieved I didn't have to try so hard anymore.

My sister continued to sit with her back straight and tall, eyes still closed, a smile still beaming across her face, and her voice unwavering. She continued to speak.

We allow you to reach into the depths of this realm and connect with the person you wish: your grandmother. First, instantly, there is a dragonfly. So strong. Over and over, there is a dragonfly skipping across the water. Now, iridescent colors. The sun is shining. There is someone peering into the water and seeing her reflection—a child. Playful, joyful, carefree, and curious.

When I heard these words, tears rolled down my face, as it further solidified my knowing that this was all real—indeed, sacred. I love dragonflies and always have. I have dragonflies everywhere. There are dragonfly pictures hanging in my home and furniture with dragonflies intricately embossed in them. I even have a tattoo on my foot that is a cross between a dragonfly and a butterfly. My guides were saying, "We're here, and we know you."

When Siri and I later processed this session, she had no clue I was so into dragonflies. We had been living in separate cities for many years, so we were rarely in each other's homes. She had no idea this would be my symbol—my proof from the spiritual guides that this was real.

Further proof came with the vision, describing the child looking into the water. For the past year, I had struggled with some of the most severe bouts of depression and anxiety I'd ever had in my life. I sought counseling and had sessions with my therapist twice a week to work through what I was experiencing. Sometimes my anxiety was so bad that as soon as I arrived at her office, I broke down crying before we could even get started. My therapist often walked me through a visualization exercise she called "calm, safe place." In this exercise, she asked me to imagine I was in a place that was very calm and safe. She never asked me to describe this place, but to think about it and really experience it in my head.

Sometimes, we spent the entire session in my calm, safe place. Being in this place brought me immediate comfort from the constant, often debilitating anxiety I was experiencing during this time. My safe place was me as a child with long curly hair, standing in the forest during a sunny day peering into the water—the exact vision my sister just explained to me. I never told anyone about my special place in my visualizations, so Siri had no idea. This was the place I had used in therapy time and time again to heal, and it was just described to me in extraordinary detail. This knowing was once again beyond anything I could have ever imagined receiving. There was no explanation. My fear completely subsided. I knew this was real, and it was a blessing.

My sister continued with the messages, now reaching out to connect with our grandmother, Nonny. She continued.

We call on grandmother. Her energy is here. Sweet, tired. Happy to connect. Eager to connect. What questions do you have for her?

I didn't know what to say. I wasn't really prepared to *say* anything. I went to speak, and my voice barely made a sound. I had wanted to speak to my grandmother for the last thirty-eight years. I *had* been speaking to my grandmother for that long, almost daily, but I never got a response—only silence. I had begged her to speak to me. To give me a sign, any sign at all, that she was listening. But I never got anything. And now it was my chance to speak to her, and I had no idea where to start. So, I said, "Are you with me?"

She is with you. She says she is not with you in the way you want or in the way you think. She is not a guardian angel or a spirit guide. She is busy doing other things, but she is available. She says if you would like to request her to be with you more, she feels that is something she could be ready for, something she could request. But she has not yet earned that place to be a guide. She is not an angel. She has not earned the place to serve that role, but she feels that she could. And with your request, she feels it's something that could happen. Would you like to make that request?

Again, I didn't know what to say. Of course, I wanted to connect with my grandmother. Of course, I wanted her to be a guide or an angel to me, whatever that meant. Silence ensued with my sister while I tried to process all of this. I tried to process the fact she hadn't really been there in heaven, watching over me all of these years the way I thought. I tried to process that she had been doing other things all of this time. I wondered what other things the guides were talking about. I wondered what all of this meant—I really did not understand. I was a little crushed she hadn't been watching over me.

I responded, simply, with, "Yes." My sister replied with my answer and suddenly became very animated and emphatic as she said these words with excitement:

It is done! It is done now, instantly and immediately. She has put in for a transfer! Siri began joyfully laughing as she said this.

She is very, very, very happy to do this and excited to do this. She does not feel worthy, but she is assured she will be guided to guide you in the way that is best for your soul. She says if you would like for it to happen, she will do the very, very, very, best she can and try to find ways to connect with you, so you know she is communicating with you. She asks because she is new at this (and not yet trained) and because you have had trouble connecting. Also, she says now is the time to come up with a symbol for which she can use to remind you she is there. What symbol would you like to choose?

I had no hesitation in answering this question. Of course, it would be a dragonfly, so that's what I said.

STORIES AND PERSPECTIVES

Then it is done! This is how she will communicate with you. It could be a real dragonfly, a picture, an image, a tattoo, a napkin. It can come in many, many forms. She asks you to remain open.

I was so happy to finally be connecting with my grandmother. My brain was working a little more now, and I could speak more clearly, so I continued communicating:

"I want to tell her I love her. I miss her, and I so wish I could have told her about my sexual abuse. I never told her. I felt like she loved me more than anything, and I really needed her love when I was little. I miss that so much. I try to be like her and cook like her and be a good person like her, and I love her."

She is with you now, holding you and hugging you and loving you, surrounding and supporting you and your healing. She understands. She would like you to know her journey as a child was not easy. Her journeys as a young adult and an older adult were not easy, either. She has a very long list of hardship and baggage longer than you know. Partially, this is what she has been busy with, working through these other things. But now she wants you to know she's with you to work through this baggage—to provide love, unconditional support, and that place of safety and healing.

She understands this is a process that will take time. She is dedicated to sharing the rest of your life with you. To her, this is no time at all. Time on the other side is so different. It is not the same as you experience it here. She says for you, you may experience time going slowly, being painful, and longing to feel her hug and embrace and love. And you may feel lonely. It is a brutal side effect of living in this realm. It is so slow. Time feels so different, and healing can feel so painful.

She says please don't ever think you are alone because you are not. You are not alone as you work through and move through the pain. Finding love and compassion for yourself and for the others in your life who were related to this event and finding forgiveness, compassion, and healing is a long and complicated process. She says she understands this path. There is no judgment. Have patience with it. She is with you in the depths for as long as it takes and in the twists and turns it takes to hold this space for you.

She wants you to know she is not alone in this with you. Your guides and angels, already in place, are making room for her to join your circle, your council. You have not been alone during any of this time, and you will not be alone moving forward. She is here as your main source. They have made room for her, and they will teach her how to connect with you. And please have patience with her, because she is new at this and she loves

― STORIES AND PERSPECTIVES ―

you very, very, very, very much. This is a big honor for her to be able to serve you in this way, and she's so tickled and just so honored that you have asked.

As I took all of this in, I asked her, "How can I connect with my guides? How can I listen to them, and how can I hear them?"

They say to color.

Color, I asked? Like artwork? Or to draw? I had always thought of myself as an artist and always loved to create. I was intrigued; this response excited me.

It is OK if you draw, but mostly, you must do something where you are not thinking. Not to stress about how beautiful your art is or what art you are creating because then you are thinking too much, and you enter a place of doubt and judgment again. They say if you use crayons and color in a coloring book, the art is already drawn, and your mind can empty—you can allow the colors to come in and those doors to open.

Also, they say you can look at art, experience colors like the sunset, or be in nature and notice the blue of the sky or the green of the grass, or the colors and shapes of the leaves on the trees.

— GUIDED —

They say for you, colors can help open you to receive the frequency of a world apart from you—a recognition of creation you did not control, and you are not in control of. Experience those things that are awe-inspiring and in which you can enjoy and immerse yourself. Something that opens your heart to say "ahhhhhh." Relinquish the busy trying of your brain. They say, do you understand?

I said, "Yes, I understand."

They say, do not try.

I said, "I have tried so hard."

And that is your mistake. Two words will take you in the opposite direction: try and hard. Neither is the path. Instead, allow and soften. Do not try. Allow. Not so hard. Softer. Allow softness. You must be gentle with yourself. And you must recognize the spirit world is not hard. It is very subtle. It is barely even there. It is like a whisper, like a feather. It is so light and so subtle. If you think too hard, you miss it, and it disintegrates. Allow yourself to be immersed in colors and imagination, in the creativity and bliss and awe of that. Separate from the stress, tension, judgment, and criticism of trying hard. Flip the coin to the opposite.

I watched my sister intensely as she delivered these messages. She appeared so calm, steady, and absolutely radiant. It all made so much sense. I had tried so very hard all of my life, often feeling like a proverbial hamster on a wheel, always trying, always going, and never stopping. They were giving me permission to stop trying so hard and to just "be," and it felt like a thousand pounds were lifted off my shoulders.

The next thing that happened during this session was one of the most incredible things I had ever experienced in my life. About six months prior to this moment, I had returned to the Catholic church after thirty years away from it. It was not a simple decision because my religious views are not always aligned with everything the church believes. I have also struggled with the widespread sexual abuse in the church, especially being a victim of sexual abuse myself. I wondered how I could be a part of something that had caused so much pain to so many others.

I decided, ultimately, no other place meant so much to me spiritually than the Catholic church. I was determined to return as a shining light to a place that was perceived as darkness by many. I decided I could be a part of the change.

The most meaningful thing to me as a Catholic has always been my relationship with the most admirable saint of the church, the Blessed Mother, Mary. My regular talks and prayers to Mary over the years in my most troubled times have always brought me a tremendous sense of peace. As we sat in the bedroom that night, my sister suddenly looked confused as she began with her next words. As she spoke, her head tilted, and she said:

Also, Mary is with you?

I said, "Mary?"

Yes. Mother Mary is with you.

Mother Mary was with me? I wondered if it was *the* Mother Mary? The one who I adored and talked to all of these years? The one I had cried to on countless nights when I felt I had no one else to turn to? The one I have kept an image of near me for my entire life to remind me of her infinite love? This was one of the most profound things I had ever heard in my life. Mother Mary was with me.

She has heard your cries and your tears, and she holds them as sacred. She is proud of the mother you are. Do not think you have not been held and heard. That is false. She has heard everything you have said and prayed, and she will continue to hear you. And now, your Nonny is within her hold. She is in her field. She is within Mary's energy. You have a team that is with you. Don't ever doubt it. And they say to write this down.

My sister stressed the words very slowly and emphatically. Write. This. Down.

They will never abandon you. They will always be there. Your team will be with you until you die. This is Mary, this is Nonny, and these are your guides. There are others: two guides and one angel. This is your team. If you feel alone and you feel they are not there, that is your own block. It is not the truth. They are there. Never will a second go by that you are alone, as long as you live. Never will a second go by that your team will leave you, or they won't hear you. That is very, very important for you to know and for you to remember. Even if you do not feel, hear, or experience them, that does not mean they have left. They are there with you always and in every second of the remainder of your years.

I asked my sister what their names were, but she was unable to grasp the names.

They will reveal themselves later. Today is not about them, but they hope you're not upset you didn't know they were there. They do not wish to reveal themselves today. Today is about knowing your Nonny is there, knowing Mary is there, and knowing your reminder is the dragonfly. That is what they want you to remember today. They say it is time to close and that you are to remember those things. And they are available for you to come back.

At that point, my sister began only speaking in the other language and stopped interpreting as the rest of the messages were not for me. She ended in silent prayer and then opened her eyes. It was over. My sister was back to just being my normal, ordinary sister. The entire session lasted almost an hour.

That was one of the most special hours I had ever experienced in my entire life. In that hour, I learned so much and experienced more healing than I had in all my years of counseling. I felt like I was finally OK to just be me. I didn't have to try so hard anymore! I was OK just the way I was. I now knew I wasn't really in control, anyway. I could just "be." I could let go. I could *soften* and *allow*. I could stop hating myself for not being perfect. I could forgive my abuser and all the people who had been involved in my abuse. I knew Mother Mary and my spirit guides and angels were with me every single moment of every single day.

That hour was one of the most sacred, special, incredible hours I have ever experienced, and the counseling I received will be with me and guide me for the rest of my life. I spent the next few months experiencing life in a completely different way. After taking care of my normal obligations, I took extra time to sit on my front porch—existing. I started going on daily walks just to experience life—the sunrise, the leaves, the grass, and everything else I did not create. It was an amazing experience. I was still a mother, a wife, and an employee, but I stopped trying so hard all the time. I gave myself permission to just be. I accepted I would never achieve perfection. It was one of the most liberating feelings I have ever experienced. I knew the universe would lead me exactly where I needed to go.

The day after my session, the dragonflies started appearing. They appeared on furniture, plates, glasses, as artwork on walls, and as real dragonflies flying around me. For four days in a row, I saw dragonflies every day. Then I saw them every once in a while, when I least expected them. I've seen more dragonflies this year than I have in my entire life. I know my Nonny is here, present, and watching over me.

And Mother Mary, my guides, and my angels are ever-present in my life. It feels subtle, yet so real.

I still have the same life and the same struggles, but now I have the comfort and faith that I am not alone, even when it feels like I am terribly alone. I know my council of guides and angels are there, doing whatever they do, although I don't understand it. I just know it. They are there, and that's all that matters. I am not alone, and I am OK. I am.

SOCIAL RESPONSIBILITIES

RATIONAL QUESTIONING

Everything described in this book occurred in earnest sincerity. Even so, I operate my life and worldview with a rational mind. In a battle to demystify these experiences, I have engaged in rational questioning. In short, how can one discern the voice of the Divine from the creativity of the psyche or from mental health disturbances?

First, considering a potential correlation between paranormal experiences and mental and emotional disturbances, were my earliest experiences with invisible friends simply a psychological coping mechanism to escape challenging family dynamics? And did my attachment to the invisible ideal stay with me to serve as an underlying psychological function throughout my adult life, manifesting as spiritual guides? My response to these questions is this: I am now a well-adjusted, healthy, productive, successful, and self-actualized adult who has found deep peace and joy in life. So maybe it worked?

Next, the channeled information moving through my mind related to concepts I was already familiar with, including meditation, prayer, energy flow, emotional regulation, projections of the mind, and embodied awareness. This contrasts with tongue-speaking Christians who report semantics related to the Holy Spirit and Christ-centered principles, while other mediums channel content that may vary still.

This begs the question: was the encrypted information generated from my own unconscious mind (or collective unconscious) rather than channeled from an omniscient source? In other words, was my sense of wholeness achieved from embracing hidden parts of the self, rather than from being graced with spiritual healing? Were the communications with angelic beings simply metaphors created from the unconscious mind, rather than true emanations of divinity? If so, did the creative intelligence of the psyche then deliver the information in a striking and other-worldly way that caused me to pay attention? And if so, what exactly drives one's psyche towards healing and wholeness? Would that be the intelligent design of God?

And then what to make of communicating with departed souls? Would that be the product of creative imagination, another function of the mind? Also, what drives others' movement towards healing when sharing these experiences? One could perceive these phenomena through the lens of a placebo effect, the power of suggestion, and the innate human desire to feel connected, seen, and heard. And if so, when the result is ultimately healing, positive, and transformative, is that a sufficiently safe and healthy outcome?

Perhaps none of my rational questions point to the truth. Perhaps in some way, they each create facets of an incomprehensible truth. Or perhaps the simplest explanation is that the unexplainable, numinous realm must remain just that: unknown. I have ultimately chosen to not only accept but to fully embrace this mystery. I have chosen to believe the supernatural is just as essential to our existence as the natural, and that our very wholeness depends on a respect for, and a surrendering to live interdependently with, this force—regardless of whether it is a phenomenon of the psyche or the spirit (or both).

In the end, I can only offer this: in a world with so much pain, anxiety, suffering, disconnection, depression, and inadequate means of coping, let us consider the incorporation of the soul in healing and the importance of one's personally-perceived spiritual journey as a core component in the development of a rich, healthy, and satisfying life.

A NASCENT FIELD

I hold reverence for honest practitioners in the healing arts, including those with the gifts of channeling and tongue-speak. Yet, I strongly believe those with these gifts also hold an enormous ethical responsibility. Unfortunately, the professions of psychics, mediums, and spiritual leaders can offer homes to frauds who prey on the vulnerabilities of consumers and followers who seek answers to life's suffering. The result is often a spoiled reputation and questionable credibility for each of these fields.

Further, a wide gap can exist between having access to psychic-spiritual gifts and fully developing these skills for professional use. I suspect well-intentioned individuals with unrefined talents can also do harm, and this is what concerns me most about my own ability. Training for licensure, internships, and/or professional supervision is not required for this work. (Of course, there are a wide variety of unregulated private training and certification programs purchasable online for anyone willing to pay.) I have searched for an established governing board, code of ethics, and scope of practice guidelines, but I have yet to find any that exist. Without them, this nascent field lacks a structure to unite, support, or hold practitioners accountable to professional integrity and to protect the public.

Most well-established professional fields today first began with little or no governance but grew over time based on public interest. Though psychic and mediumship abilities have likely been around since the beginning of humankind, and though there are considerable scientific and legal hurdles to overcome, this underdeveloped field may still have the potential to develop legitimacy and professionalism. The ethical standards, scope of practice guidelines, and licensure requirements outlined by other professional associations may provide a general model for the field. And a neutral, non-profit, overarching accrediting body providing credentialing for those practicing mystical-psychic mediumship (tongue-speak or otherwise) could change the landscape dramatically.

CONCLUSION

ONE BEAUTIFUL AND AWKWARD DAY AT A TIME

Do not confuse sacredness. Do not confuse what is holy with what is mundane. All energies are equal. They are one. The mundane is sacred. The struggle is holy.

My journey may be unique in some ways, but I am not special. Every one of us can connect with the small, still voice of our soul and with a magnificent power greater than ourselves. We can each surrender a little more ego and live with a little more love in our lives. And every one of us has the ability to choose a life of courageous authenticity, no matter how unusual we are. If and when we make that step, life continues to unfold with mostly mundane moments that somehow become threaded with awe-inspiring golden sparks of joy and aliveness.

This week, I analyzed data, created a beautiful spreadsheet, and collaborated in a business meeting. I exchanged energy and information through countless emails and conference calls. I smiled when I saw the twinkle in a stranger's eyes as he played his guitar on the edge of a grassy patch in a parking lot. I made love with my husband. I hiked in the mountains with friends, and we crunched colorful autumn leaves on the rooted and rocky path up to a breezy waterfall in the Smoky Mountains. This week I also spoke in tongues, received guided messages, and felt immense inner peace and clarity. I marveled at the outstretched wings of a red-tail hawk soaring high in the baby blue sky. I was guided by the visions in my dreams. I sent light-filled prayers to those I love and also to those in my life with whom I struggle. I danced in the kitchen. I baked tofu. I piddled around the house.

I rummaged around my bathroom closet and grew irritated with its dark and cluttered chaos. So, I installed a battery-operated light directly onto the wall. The dim, cramped space became suddenly illuminated, and memories from the past stared down at me from the shelves: a giant bottle of Advil for the headaches, Omeprazole for the stomach ulcers, and lidocaine patches for the back pain. They were all reminders of the misery I endured before finally surrendering—before accepting and honoring my complete nature. The memories brought up sadness for that part of my journey. But they also brought an appreciation for the wisdom of the human body and how it distinctly communicates essential imbalances. Standing there in the bathroom, a tinge of hope hit me. The human spirit is resilient. It can move through states of suffering and disconnection and come out the other side stronger and more whole.

After cleaning out the expired medications and organizing the shelves, my eyes fell to the floor of the closet, where a scale was coated in dust. I pulled it out, wiped it off, and stepped on the teal and grey glass square. The years of hiding behind screens and substances caught up with me and were now reflected in the numbers on the digital display.

Just as my ego glimpses the illusion that maybe I'm arriving as a self-actualized and enlightened being, the universe reminds me humility is my path forward. There is always another layer to attend to. The prescription bottle of anti-inflammatory pills on my bedside table was now coming to mind. I was still recovering from a complicated knee surgery (the consequence of my ambitious ice-skating regimen), but that surgery was two years ago at this point. The last several years of pro-inflammatory indulgences and the resulting extra pounds I now carried were worsening the swollen pain. I started my career as a nutritionist who guided others in weight management, and beyond addressing the inflammation and nutrition, this pointed to perhaps the most difficult underlying pattern to admit—the gap between knowing and doing, words and actions, hypocrisy and truth. So, the journey towards self-awareness, self-compassion, and honest self-care continues, with the sobering recognition that arrival is not a likely outcome in this lifetime.

So far, it has taken decades to honor, discern, and learn from what were once indiscernible utterings—yet have developed into soulful, sage instructions. It has taken many years to soften the unyielding grip of my threatened ego, shed the armor of my hardened heart, and dissolve the illusion of duality between the mundane and sacred elements of the human experience. It has taken my entire forty-four years of life to learn how to love myself and others—to realize that truth and love are powerful healers, and choosing wholehearted self-acceptance may be one of the hardest and most powerful gifts we can give to ourselves.

The journey to get to this point has taken longer than I expected, requiring far more tolerance and resilience than I would have once thought to be reasonable. I am grateful to have made it through the dark years of fear, anxiety, depression, and isolation, though I recognize these intense teachers may resurface again in the future. For now, I rest in the acceptance of what is and what I am today. I accept my awkward, amazing truth as a formless soul with evolving consciousness who bears the spiritual gift of tongue-speaking mediumship and the professional gift of business leadership.

With professional roots grounded in research and ethical integrity, I dream of a robust (if not miraculous) multi-disciplinary group comprised of scientists, practitioners, mental health leaders, physical healers, and spiritual leaders coming together with the same goal: to establish legitimacy and accountability for an integrative approach to healing, including the mystical-psychic phenomenon of mediumship. The paradoxical conundrum is that we cannot explain that which is unexplainable, we cannot bind that which is boundless, and we cannot prove that which is only perceptible to those who believe it exists.

We are each one being with access to multiple dimensions guiding us toward our full human potential. The soul is vast and endless. The ego is actively on guard, yet also necessary to befriend. The body is a rich source of information along the path towards self-awareness, and the psyche works creatively towards permeability across ordinary and extraordinary states of consciousness. The spiritual realm is available, loving, and supportive, should we choose to open ourselves to receive it. Life is a continuum of all things seen and unseen, dancing and interacting as one reality, revealing itself to us as we reveal ourselves to it.

I pray for my continued becoming, and I pray for yours as well. May you courageously journey into the unknown, accessing all available dimensions of knowledge and guidance to move you towards healing and wholeness. And may you ultimately find peaceful acceptance of, and love for, the truly awkward and amazing being that you are.

ACKNOWLEDGMENTS

A gigantic thank you to Annie. Thank you for helping me embrace the beauty and mystery of this experience and contributing your perspectives to this book. The countless Saturdays spent on your back porch provided the incubator of safety to nurture my soul into awakening. Our friendship is one of the greatest blessings in my life. I am eternally grateful for your partnership in this journey, for which no words can adequately express.

A very special thank you to Laura for your patient transcription work over the years to discern the English from the tongue-speak. This book would not have been possible without you.

Thank you, Blake, for expressing your soulful nature, which invited me to do the same. You taught me to value human connection as much as achievements and to sense what lies beyond pretenses and facades (especially my own). Thank you for your grace, patience, and humility these past ten years, which helped to balance my very nature.

Thanks to all of my friends and colleagues in recovery. Both individually and collectively, your courage to surrender and live each day in raw vulnerability is an unending source of inspiration.

Thank you, Mom and Dad, for unconditionally loving and supporting my uniqueness in every stage of life, and especially during the last few years of this journey as you non-judgmentally held the space for my spirit to come out of hiding. Thank you, Dad, for modeling joyous living. Thank you, Mom, for contributing your perspectives to this book.

Thank you, Kerry, Anne-Marie, and Ali, my sisters, for your love and acceptance, even in my darkest, most isolated years. Thank you, Kerry, for contributing your perspectives to this book.

Thanks also to Michelle, Missy, and Annie, my soul sisters, with whom miracles are always possible. And the same to Mary, the bearer of magic.

To my daughters, Raminder and Sara, thank you for bringing me endless joy and also for the opportunity to

ACKNOWLEDGMENTS

practice unconditional love. Thank you for calling out my hypocrisies and for always encouraging me to choose real happiness over existence in a soul-crushing, societally-constructed box. You are precious teachers.

And to my beloved husband, Michael, thank you for your tenacity so we could return to tender, genuine love. Thank you for honoring your own life path, which inspired me to do the same. I am forever grateful that through our differences, we have found oneness.

RECOMMENDED READINGS

Here is a list of publications I have appreciated along my journey; however, this is in no way meant to be a comprehensive summary of the topics mentioned in the book.

AUTHENTIC, COMPASSIONATE, & COURAGEOUS LIVING

- *Big Magic: Creative Living Beyond Fear* by Elizabeth Gilbert
- *Braving the Wilderness: The Quest for True Belonging and the Courage to Stand Alone* by Brené Brown, PhD
- *Midlife and the Great Unknown* by David Whyte

- *Self-Compassion: The Proven Power of Being Kind to Yourself* by Kristin Neff
- *The Hero with a Thousand Faces* by Joseph Campbell
- *The Gifts of Imperfection: Let Go of Who You Think You're Supposed to Be and Embrace Who You Are* by Brené Brown, PhD
- *What to Remember When Waking: The Disciplines of an Everyday Life* by David Whyte
- *Untamed* by Glennon Doyle

CHANNELING, TONGUE-SPEAK, SHAMANISM, SYMBOLISM AND NON-ORDINARY STATES OF CONSCIOUSNESS

- *Believe, Ask, Act: Divine Steps to Raise Your Intuition, Create Change, and Discover Happiness* by MaryAnn DiMarco
- *How to Change Your Mind: What the New Science of Psychedelics Tells Us Consciousness, Dying, Addiction, Depression, and Transcendence* by Michael Pollan
- *Imagery in Healing: Shamanism and Modern Medicine* by Jeanne Achterberg, PhD
- *Jaguar in the Body Butterfly in the Heart* by Ya'Acov Darling Khan

— RECOMMENDED READINGS —

- *Man and His Symbols* by Carl G. Jung, MD
- *Speaking in Tongues: A Cross-Cultural Study of Glossolalia* by Felicitas D. Goodman, PhD
- *The Flip: Epiphanies of Mind and the Future of Knowledge* by Jeffrey J. Kripal, PhD
- *The Wisdom of the Shamans: What the Ancient Masters Can Teach Us About Love and Life* by Don Jose Ruiz
- *Trancework: An Introduction to the Practice of Clinical Hypnosis* by Michael Yapko, PhD
- *With the Tongues of Men and Angels: A Study of Channeling* by Arthur Hastings, PhD

EGO SURRENDER & SPIRITUAL DEVELOPMENT

- *A Course in Miracles* by Helen Schucman, PhD
- *Broken Open: How Difficult Times Can Help Us Grow* by Elizabeth Lesser
- *Tao Te Ching: The Book of the Way* by Lao Tzu
- *The Book of Joy* by His Holiness the Dalai Lama, Desmond Tutu, and Douglas Abrams
- *The Places That Scare You: A Guide to Fearlessness in Difficult Times* by Pema Chödrön
- *The Universe Has Your Back: Transform Fear to Faith* by Gabrielle Bernstein

- *The Untethered Soul: The Journey Beyond Yourself* by Michael A. Singer
- *When Things Fall Apart: Heart Advice for Difficult Times* by Pema Chödrön

MIND-BODY MEDICINE & NEUROBIOLOGY IN HEALING

- *Full Catastrophe Living: Using the Wisdom of Your Body and Mind to Face Stress, Pain, and Illness* by Jon Kabat-Zinn, PhD
- *In an Unspoken Voice: How the Body Releases Trauma and Restores Goodness* by Peter Levine, PhD
- *Manifesto for a New Medicine: Your Guide to Healing Partnerships and the Wise Use of Alternative Therapies* by James Gordon, MD
- *Mindfulness and the Brain* by Jack Kornfield and Daniel Siegel, MD
- *Molecules of Emotion: The Science Behind Mind-Body Medicine* by Candace B. Pert, PhD
- *My Stroke of Insight: A Brain Scientist's Personal Journey* by Jill Bolte Taylor, PhD
- *The Body Keeps the Score: Brain, Mind, and Body in the Healing of Trauma* by Bessel Van Der Kolk, MD

— RECOMMENDED READINGS —

- *The Divided Mind: The Epidemic of Mindbody Disorders* by John Sarno, MD
- *The Polyvagal Theory: Neurophysiological Foundations of Emotions, Attachment, Communication, Self-Regulation* by Stephen W. Porges
- *Unstuck: Your Guide to the Seven-Stage Journey Out of Depression* by James Gordon, MD
- *Wired for Joy: A Revolutionary Method for Creating Happiness from Within* by Laurel Mellin, PhD

NEAR-DEATH EXPERIENCES & REINCARNATION

- *Life Before Life: Children's Memories of Previous Lives* by Jim Tucker, MD
- *Many Lives, Many Masters: The True Story of a Prominent Psychiatrist, His Young Patient, and the Past-Life Therapy That Changed Both Their Lives* by Brian Weiss, MD
- *Messages from the Masters: Tapping into the Power of Love* by Brian Weiss, MD
- *Miracles Happen: The Transformational Healing Power of Past-Life Memories* by Brian Weiss, MD
- *Proof of Heaven: A Neurosurgeon's Journey into the Afterlife* by Eben Alexander, MD

ABOUT THE AUTHOR

Siri K. Zemel, PhD, holds a doctorate in mind-body medicine with a concentration in healthcare systems. Dr. Zemel has served in behavioral healthcare leadership for the past fifteen years and recently embraced her lifelong gift as a spiritual medium. With a master's degree in nutrition science, she began her early career as a dietitian. She was raised Catholic, converted to Sikhism, married a Jew, and then retired from organized religion altogether. Dr. Zemel is an advocate for integrative healing, including the incorporation of mystical experiences alongside traditional physical and mental healthcare.

www.ingramcontent.com/pod-product-compliance
Lightning Source LLC
Chambersburg PA
CBHW060523080526
44586CB00012B/593